I0823570

PRAISE FOR

WHY CAN'T THEY BE LIKE ME?

"The perfect primer on executive coaching—when you need it, why it works, and how it can transform your life. *Why Can't They Be Like Me?* shows you exactly what it's like to supercharge your leadership with an excellent executive coach. Feedback is the breakfast of champions—and as this book shows, feedback from the right coach is invaluable."

—Ken Blanchard, coauthor of *The One Minute Manager®*

"This book is a mirror that high achievers can't look away from. It's bold, funny, and painfully real—because the hardest leadership lesson isn't about strategy or execution. It's about you."

—JD Meier, executive coach, author, and former innovation coach to Satya Nadella

"If you want to get a look at the real value of coaching, read *Why Can't They Be Like Me?* It's a fresh take on how leaders can navigate their blind spots and achieve breakthrough performance. I highly recommend!"

—Alisa Cohn, author of *From Start-Up to Grown-Up*

"**OOOO**, *that's* how it works! A compelling and timeless story that you won't be able to put down on how to grow as a leader through **O**penness to change, **O**penness to feedback, **O**penness to action, and **O**penness to accountability, by the world's best."

—David Noble, leadership coach and senior advisor to Egon Zehnder and the Institute of Coaching

"A refreshingly real and relevant parable! The book's insight for becoming a coachable leader will help those looking to achieve breakthrough performance. A rare business book that you'll want to read in one sitting!"

—Sanyin Siang, Duke University professor and Thinkers50 Hall of Fame inductee

"A great exploration of what it truly takes to transform as a leader. The book's portrayal of the coaching relationship feels authentic and nuanced, offering readers a clear picture of both the challenges and rewards of executive coaching. Essential reading for any leader considering working with a coach."

—Mark Thompson, *New York Times* bestselling author, Thinkers50 legend, and world's #1 CEO coach

"This compelling parable does what the best leadership books do: it holds up a mirror and refuses to let you look away. It brilliantly exposes the uncomfortable truth that success can become our greatest trap—the world's most accomplished leaders are often the most blind to their need for change. Díaz-Ortiz and Goldsmith's raw, honest story will resonate with any leader brave enough to face the crisis within and transform their greatest nemesis into their most powerful ally."

—Connie Dieken, senior executive coach and founder of The Influence Lab

"This book is essential reading for coaches and executives who want a front-row seat to how real transformative coaching takes place. It reveals how change unfolds—not in a straight line, but through a powerful ripple effect that elevates not just the leader being coached, but also everyone around them."

—Jennifer Goldman-Wetzler, PhD, executive coach, and bestselling author of *Optimal Outcomes: Free Yourself from Conflict at Work, at Home, and in Life*

"Marshall Goldsmith and Claire Díaz-Ortiz have written a terrific short book that anyone even considering being coached—or even simply the coaching-curious—should read. Eminently readable, the compelling story that they tell is a page-turner that teaches as much as it entertains."

—Peter Bregman, CEO of Bregman Partners and bestselling author of *18 Minutes* and *Leading with Emotional Courage*

"This compelling parable does what the best leadership books do: it holds up a mirror and refuses to let you look away. It brilliantly exposes the uncomfortable truth that success can become our greatest trap—the world's most accomplished leaders are often the most blind to their need for change. Díaz-Ortiz and Goldsmith's raw, honest story will resonate with any leader brave enough to face the crisis within and transform their greatest nemesis into their most powerful ally."

—Connie Dieken, senior executive coach and founder of The Influence Lab

"This book is essential reading for coaches and executives who want a front-row seat to how real transformative coaching takes place. It reveals how change unfolds—not in a straight line, but through a powerful ripple effect that elevates not just the leader being coached, but also everyone around them."

—Jennifer Goldman-Wetzler, PhD, executive coach and bestselling author of *Optimal Outcomes: Free Yourself from Conflict at Work, at Home, and in Life*

"Marshall Goldsmith and Claire Díaz-Ortiz have written a terrific short book that anyone even considering being coached—or even simply the coaching-curious—should read. Eminently readable, the compelling story that they tell is a page-turner that teaches as much as it entertains."

—Peter Bregman, CEO of Bregman Partners and bestselling author of *18 Minutes* and *Leading with Emotional Courage*

"What happens when success becomes your biggest obstacle? This masterful story follows a Silicon Valley CEO's humbling transformation through executive coaching. Díaz-Ortiz and Goldsmith deliver a captivating parable about growth, resilience, and becoming truly coachable."

—Claudius A. Hildebrand, leadership coach and coauthor of *The Life Cycle of a CEO*

"Developing as a leader is hard, especially when you don't have a guide or a coach. Well, *Why Can't They Be Like Me?* can be your guide, showing how the fresh perspective on the purpose and practicality of powerful executive coaching can help you become the leader you want to be, and the one your people deserve. Enjoy the read, enjoy the journey."

—Chester Elton, bestselling author of *The Carrot Principle*, *Anxiety at Work*, and *Leading with Gratitude*

amplifypublishinggroup.com
publishing.100coaches.com

Why Can't They Be Like Me?

For more information, please contact:
100 Coaches Publishing, an imprint of Amplify Publishing Group
620 Herndon Parkway, Suite 220
Herndon, VA 20170
info@amplifypublishing.com

Library of Congress Control Number: 2025911221

CPSIA Code: PRV0925A

ISBN-13: 979-8-89138-262-6

Printed in the United States

A PARABLE OF SHIFTING PERSPECTIVES

CLAIRE DIAZ-ORTIZ
MARSHALL GOLDSMITH

CONTENTS

FOREWORD XI

PART 1
OPEN TO CHANGE XV

PART 2
OPEN TO FEEDBACK. 55

PART 3
OPEN TO ACTION 99

PART 4
OPEN TO ACCOUNTABILITY. 159

APPENDIX. 175

ABOUT THIS BOOK 179

ABOUT THE AUTHORS. 181

ABOUT 100 COACHES 183

FOREWORD

Why can't they be like me?

It's a question that has crossed all of our minds at one point or another. After all, our own methods, perspectives, and decision-making processes have brought us success and propelled us into leadership positions. Why wouldn't we want some of our strongest attributes mirrored back to us by our colleagues and across our organization?

But herein lies one of leadership's greatest paradoxes: the very thinking that drives us to seek out carbon copies of ourselves is often what limits our organization's potential for innovation, growth, and sustainable success. True leadership excellence, we've discovered, lies not in replication but in recognition—recognition of the inimitable value that each individual brings to the table.

As longtime collaborators of Marshall and Claire, we've had the distinct privilege of witnessing firsthand how this mindset manifests across various leadership contexts. Through our work deploying the world's most elite executive coaches to serve value-creating leaders, we've observed time and again how the desire for conformity can inadvertently stifle the very creativity and innovation that organizations need to thrive.

We experienced this in our early days of working together. Our contrasting styles were immediately apparent. Where one saw the big picture, the other focused on crucial details. When one wanted to move quickly, the other insisted on building sustainable processes. One's enthusiasm for new possibilities was often met with the other's careful consideration of risks. Over time, we learned to lean into our different perspectives. The result wasn't just better decisions—it was a powerful new way of leading together in partnership.

In those early days, either of us could have asked, "Why can't they be like me?" Instead, we asked a different question: "What if these differing viewpoints are exactly what we need?" That shift in perspective changed everything. We discovered that leadership isn't about finding replicas of ourselves—it's about creating partnerships that complement and challenge us.

Our experiences learning and charting new waters together have shaped our shared understanding of leadership. We've seen how the most effective leaders aren't those who try to clone themselves, but those who actively seek out and embrace varying approaches and different strengths in others. They understand that their way—however successful it's been—is just one piece of a larger puzzle. Learning how to partner well with others and tap into their intrinsic motivations is key to creating a sustainable movement. It's essential to building a company that scales.

In their varying ways, Marshall and Claire have long championed this truth, highlighting how the very qualities that drive individual success can become limitations when imposed on others. This book builds on the foundation that Marshall laid in his perennial bestseller *What Got You Here Won't Get You There,* in which he reveals why the very habits that have contributed to a person's success may be the same ones holding them back from achieving greater heights.

Through the combined wisdom of Marshall's decades of coaching experience, Claire's innovative insights, and the practical applications we've witnessed through our work at 100 Coaches Agency, this book provides a road map to embracing differences rather than seeking to eliminate them. Through storytelling, it pulls back the curtain on the thoughts, feelings, and process we've seen many executives work through in the coaching process. At the top of organizations, it takes a quantum leap in leadership to reach the next rung on the ladder. *Why Can't They Be Like Me?* expounds key lessons from the many who have made the leap before you.

The path forward, we believe, isn't about molding others in our image. It's about creating spaces where every individual's unique contribution is recognized, valued, and integrated into a greater whole that is more than the sum of its parts. This is the transformative power of embracing difference: Together, it allows us to achieve results that would be impossible through homogeneity alone.

As you journey through these pages, we invite you to challenge your own assumptions about leadership and success. Consider how the very differences that sometimes frustrate you might actually be the key to unlocking new possibilities. After all, the most powerful partnerships between exceptional personalities and perspectives don't just add—they multiply.

Scott Osman and Jacquelyn Lane
Cofounders, 100 Coaches Agency
Coauthors, *Becoming Coachable*

PART 1

OPEN TO CHANGE

CHAPTER 1

"Everything would have been fine if it hadn't been for Jerry," Todd Turner said as the plane started its descent into Vancouver.

"Jerry?" This time, the woman in the seat next to him barely looked up.

They'd been talking a lot on the twelve-hour flight from Dubai. Well, Todd had been talking. Since breakfast, he'd been telling the woman about Jerry, the graphic designer tasked with the most important presentation deck of Todd's life. Jerry was good at his job, of course. Not many people working at one of the hottest companies in Silicon Valley were blatantly bad at their jobs. But it took Jerry so long to do things. He was just so methodical.

"He's too much of a perfectionist," Todd said. "Sometimes, Jerry needs to break things."

"Break things?"

They had landed now, and the woman was unbuckling her seat belt, checking her seatback pocket. Todd thought she could be paying more attention.

"You know what I sometimes think?" he said.

The woman winced as she yanked down her carry-on from the overhead bin. It was heavy. Todd spoke to the back of her head as she walked away.

"Why can't they all be like me?"

●■▲

Todd knew his TED talk had not gone well. There had been applause, of course, everyone had to applaud. But he hadn't become one of the hottest entrepreneurs of the past decade without being able to read a room. Agreeing to do the talk in the first place had been a risk. TED talks were known for their soul-baring arcs of redemption: the lower the pit, the higher the rise. But Todd hadn't wanted to do all that. "Let's just focus on our wins," he had said to the team at LUNAQ when they were helping him craft the talk. In the corner, LUNAQ's CMO had let out a strangled, high-pitched noise. Todd had barreled ahead. He was the CEO. It was his call. And now that it was over, he had to accept the results. He had done what he could do. You can't win them all, he told himself.

After the speeches, he had a quick thirty minutes in his hotel room to fire off a few emails before he got back in the black car to go to the speakers' dinner.

"You don't have to go," his executive assistant told him.

He knew that, obviously. He rarely went to these things. He flew in, he flew out, he flew somewhere else again. He was a big deal, after all. Ten years after starting LUNAQ in his basement, his company now had more than a thousand employees and was a unicorn several times over. To fuel his rapid growth, and to meet the needs of businesses everywhere clambering for more of his company's innovative software solutions, he'd raised hundreds of millions of dollars in venture capital funding. Along the way, he'd graced the cover of many a business magazine with the story of his gritty rise to success. But this was TED. The *mainstage*. All the speakers were big deals; it was worth going to the dinner.

There was also the other thing. He pushed any thought of it out of his mind. It was not a good time to think about the other thing.

"All the other speakers are going," he told his executive assistant. "I'm going to go." He didn't elaborate.

He was the last to arrive at the dinner, which was taking place in an industrial warehouse that appeared to have recently emerged from an apocalypse. Most of the cavernous space was dark and empty. In the center, there were strange, sparkly green lights that dripped down like seaweed from the high ceilings onto a long, wrought-iron table. As he got closer, he looked up and stared. Was this art? That was when the hosts greeted him warmly, leading him to his name card at the end of the long table.

He was seated across from a child. She was the prodigy, the one who'd built the robot to scale up the new malaria vaccines. Her talk had been the biggest hit of the year. If you could call the performance a talk. It had been more like a ventriloquist's act, a musical one, with the kid, and the robot, singing about blood. The kid hadn't just built the medical robot, which now was being dropped into countries all over Africa, she had also created one of the most popular live-streaming social media accounts in the world. They had debuted a new song, "Splat," on the TED stage, and the robot had sung, "My blood is your blood is our blood..."

The seating placement was an exciting development. All smiles, Todd went in for a high five.

"I can't get your song out of my head. My kids love you! Too bad there's no malaria in Palo Alto!"

"Gaming," the kid said. "Not interacting."

Deflated, Todd sat down. Next to him, one of the first astronauts to land on the moon had fallen asleep. It was late for old people, Todd thought as he looked down the table in search of someone to talk to. A former vice president was sitting next to the woman who had broken the world record for ice diving. They had given great talks, and they were laughing rowdily as a man with curly white hair refilled their glasses. He wasn't the waiter.

"Who's that?" Todd said to the kid. She didn't look up.

By the second course, a vegan one in honor of the Nigerian Paralympian turned climate change activist, Todd was sick of looking at the kid tapping on her screen. If he had wanted that, he could have stayed home. For a second, his mind flashed back to his house. Had he talked to his wife and kids since he'd left Dubai? He couldn't remember. All the days were beginning to run together.

He'd have to take matters into his own hands. Todd stood up from the table and walked down to the other end.

"Hi," he said. "I'm Todd Turner. It looks like you're the folks having all the fun. Can I sit?"

"We know who you are!" the man with white hair said. Had he given a talk today? If so, Todd hadn't seen it. "Come join us!"

The white-haired man poured out another round. Todd held out his glass.

CHAPTER 2

When Todd woke the next morning, the night before felt like a strange dream. The seaweed lights, the karaoke, the vodka shots in the former vice president's suite. One thing he knew for sure was that he hadn't been up that late in a long time. But what had really happened last night? He pulled out his phone to check for hard evidence. There he was, taking a selfie with the former vice president. Next to them, the white-haired guy was pouring champagne into the mouth of the malaria robot.

The white-haired guy hadn't just been a hanger-on as Todd had suspected. He had seen people like that. Barnacles, he called them. They stayed close to wealthy celebrities, high-flying corporate executives, hot politicians. They laughed at everything. They never picked up the tab. But Ray de Luca was not a barnacle. Not even close. Because Ray de Luca was the glue that held all of these chaotic personalities together. He was the one person at the table everyone loved.

"Without Ray, I would never have been able to negotiate that peace treaty," the vice president had said. Todd knew the one. It had earned the vice president the Nobel Peace Prize.

“Without his book, I would never have gone back to diving at sixty,” the ice diver had said.

“Which one?” the vice president had said. It turned out that there were dozens. Ray de Luca had sold twenty million books.

“Thirty million!” the child prodigy had said. “His last book was life-changing. After I read it, my career transformed.” She’d been nine.

It had taken a long time for anyone to tell Todd exactly what this guy did.

“But what is his *job*?” Todd had said. Todd hadn’t understood any of the euphemisms that the speakers had used: *He transformed leaders, he made me a new person, he saved my life.*

“He’s an executive coach,” the vice president had said. “They say he’s the best in the world. I tend to agree.” Todd had looked skeptical. He had tried coaches. They’d helped him some, but not *that* much. He had said as much to the vice president.

“Sounds like you haven’t had a great one,” the vice president had said.

● ■ ▲

Todd was back on the plane before breakfast. The flight attendants had already told him to put his cell phone on airplane mode when he pulled it out of his pocket and fired it up again. He’d vacillated back and forth all morning trying to decide if he should reach out, but he must have met Ray de Luca for a reason. He sat in his seat as the gray rain of Vancouver pounded against the little airplane window. He texted Ray.

It was great to meet you last night. I wanted to ask if I could call you sometime. To be honest, I’m in a bit of a bind.

He immediately erased the last sentence and tried again.

I was thinking I could use some help thinking through something that's been on my mind. Nope, that wouldn't work either.

Finally, he settled on, *I'd love to catch up.*

He hit send before he had time to regret it. Catch up on what? They'd just met!

By the time they took off, Ray had already texted back. *Call me on Sunday? I'll be on the water. I'll pick up then.*

CHAPTER 3

When Sunday came, Todd called Ray. True to his word, Ray picked up. Todd could hear wind and shrieking. It didn't sound good.

"Hold on," Ray said. Now he was yelling at somebody. "What did I tell you last time? Do not throw Floppy Cat in the water!" Ray was back. "Grandkids," he said. "Three of them. One's a little devil."

"Devil grandfather!" A high-pitched voice shouted back.

"But you never know which one," Ray said.

"Is this a bad time?" Todd said.

"Not at all," Ray said. "Just let me go down to the cabin." Todd heard a door slam and then the click of a lock.

"Are the kids okay up there…on the deck? With their… toy cat?" Todd asked.

"Oh, it's a real cat," Ray said. "Anyway, the boat's got a captain. And the kids have a father. Glad I don't have their jobs." Ray laughed at his own joke.

Todd took a sip of water, recalibrating. The chaos now behind them, he explained to Ray why he was calling.

Something was very broken at LUNAQ, and he didn't know how to put it back together again. Could Ray help?

Todd started in on a long story.

Ray cut him off. "Oh no, no, no. *Absolutely not!* I don't do that kind of stuff anymore. I can't be all…tied down. These days, I'm a free-range chicken."

"You're a chicken?"

"A free-range one! I'm in the Super Bowl of life!"

Despite himself, Todd laughed. He thought for the hundredth time since meeting him, *Who was this guy?* He was about to say something else when he heard loud banging on Ray's end. Someone with a deep voice was yelling about a cat.

"Sounds like I need to put this father of theirs on a performance plan," Ray said. "Now, when are you coming to San Diego for karaoke?"

CHAPTER 4

Todd wasn't used to hearing "no." After hanging up the phone, he immediately texted his assistant.

I need to get to San Diego this week, he said. *And please find the best place to do karaoke.*

Karaoke? She texted back.

It's a long story.

Four days later, Todd was ringing the doorbell of a large, modern home. A petite woman with a shock of bright pink hair opened the door.

"Hello!" she said. "You must be Todd. Come on in." She gestured forward, and Todd stepped through the door. "I'm painting."

Todd could see that. As he walked inside, he saw that the entire two-story great room was covered from top to bottom with shelves full of painting supplies and filled with a jumble of tables. Massive canvases draped in paint-speckled sheets leaned against all available wall spaces.

"Wow," he said. "And you do it right here…in the living room?" He was trying to be tactful.

"Ha!" she said. "This isn't the living room. This is my studio. As Ray says, sometimes what looks like the front door is not the front door at all." Something about the way she said it made Todd wonder if he should be writing this down. "Come on in. I'll take you to Ray."

Along the way, he met the housekeeper, who followed them with a tray of coffee and cakes. They were in a hallway at the far side of the house when Todd began to hear the voices. One was loud and booming, the other was softer and insistent. Strangely, they both sounded like Ray. The door at the end of the hall was open, and Todd, Ray's wife, and the housekeeper walked in together.

Inside, Ray was talking.

To Ray.

"I can't be expected to be in Seoul on Tuesday and Buenos Aires on Wednesday," the Ray who Todd had met said. Ray was sitting in an imposing purple armchair, his arms on the armrests.

The other Ray, whose face was being streamed from a large computer monitor mounted on a moveable trolley, responded. "I can do Buenos Aires. I'd love the chance to practice my Spanish. *Vamos a la playa, loco.*" Todd wasn't certain, but it looked like the robot had just done a little dance.

"Oh look, cake!" Grinning widely, the Ray in the armchair got up to take the tray from the housekeeper. Then he went to open a wooden door to reveal a glass refrigerator full of small bottles in a rainbow of colors. Looking at Todd this time, he pulled one out. "Small-batch kombucha from the Willamette Valley." He pointed to his stomach. "My gut microbiome."

Todd's eyes went from one Ray to the other. It was a lot to take in. "Uh, who's your friend?" Todd said as he pointed to the computer monitor on wheels.

Pouring out the kombucha into glasses, Ray explained, “That’s Raybot. Raybot, say, hello.”

“Hello, intruders,” said the Ray on the monitor. “I’m Ray 2.0.”

“So that makes you…Ray 1.0?” Todd said to the Ray handing him a glass of bubbly.

“Oh, Todd, there is so much to tell you!” Ray put his arm around Todd’s shoulder and ushered him to a seat on the couch. Once Ray was back in the purple chair, he told Todd about how a burgeoning interest in artificial intelligence had led him to hire a small team of researchers to teach him everything he needed to know about the topic. One guy’s job was just to read about the best ways AI was being used in far-flung industries and to tell Ray about them. “I’m old, Todd, but that doesn’t mean I only need the CliffsNotes version of events. I can see how big AI is going to be for the coaching world.”

He then summarized the past year of experimenting with his tech team to get Raybot just right. “Eventually, I did a test. I set up a video call for Raybot with my daughter, and ten minutes in she said, ‘Dad, I don’t want to listen to your BS today. Don’t I get enough of this at Sunday dinners?’ She had no idea it wasn’t me!”

It was a learning journey, of course, Ray said, and they were always making improvements. “But he’s already smarter than I am. And he’s almost better looking! His attitude is still a work in progress.” By now, Ray’s glass was empty. He looked at Todd’s. “Drink up! Karaoke!”

Todd cleared his throat. “Before we head out, I wanted to talk to you about something. As I said on the phone, I’m at a major crossroads with LUNAQ, and I could really use some advice. I know how helpful you've been to other leaders in times of crisis—"

Ray cut him off. "Oh no, we're not getting into all that again. I already told you. These days, I'm free-range."

"Right…the chicken. Well, I just thought…and since money is no object—"

"Money?" Ray said. "This is not about money." Ray looked at Todd. "Can I ask you a question? Did you really come to San Diego to convince me to be your executive coach?"

Todd was honest, "Maybe?"

"And is that generally how you get what you want in life? By trying to convince people to do things they don't want to do?" Ray said.

For a moment, Todd was taken aback. He raised his two hands in equanimity, "Yeah?"

"That might be something you're going to want to work on with Cora."

Now Todd was confused all over again. Every moment in the presence of Ray de Luca was proving increasingly confounding. "Is Cora another Robot?"

"Not exactly," Ray said.

"But close!" Raybot added.

Cora was a former executive at a big tech company. Like LUNAQ, the company had started small, and Cora had been there from the beginning, rising through the ranks and eventually leaving to focus on her true zone of genius: coaching other leaders. Ray explained that part of his free-range retirement was to closely mentor a handful of younger executive coaches to become the next him. That way, when people asked him to do things he didn't want to do anymore, he could recommend one of them for the job.

"So, you can't help me?" Todd said.

"Todd, let me explain something. I've spent my career as a coach focused on behavioral change. Coaches like Cora, one of the best I've ever mentored, aren't here to hand you a new strategy or give you a quick fix. She only gets paid if what she does works. And since she is going to be even better than I could be, she is going to be very rich! But behavioral change takes time. It also takes work. Is this really something you are motivated to take on?"

"It's different from what I thought it was, I admit. But at this point, I'll do anything. And I know I have some behaviors that could use help. Sometimes I can come across too strong, for example."

"That could be a potential behavior to look at. First, you and Cora will decide on the key behavioral issues that you want to fix. The one or two or three behavioral changes that will produce the most positive transformation in your life. Next, you will determine who the stakeholders are to decide if the change happened. Those are the people the coach talks to at the beginning of the engagement to best understand how you're really coming across in the world and the people we talk to at the end to see if our work together has made a difference. Does that make sense?"

"It does, but what about fixing my crisis?"

"Well, that's the thing," said Ray. "When leaders come with urgent issues, they often think the answer lies in a quick external change. They are usually wrong. That's because what got you here won't get you there. Cora is going to help you understand all that."

"But wait, how much C-suite experience does she really have?" Todd said.

"First, you're trying to convince me to work with you, and now you're questioning my judgment?" Ray laughed. "Raybot, can you believe this guy?"

The robot shook his head. "That might be something else you want to work on with Cora," Raybot said. "I hope you like beverages!"

CHAPTER 5

Over the next week, Todd thought about what Ray had asked him. Did he have the motivation to take on behavioral coaching? When he first reached out to Ray, he was looking for a quick fix. But what if what Ray said was true, that the biggest things holding him back were internal? That would explain why his earlier attempts at strategic coaching hadn't done much. Todd had always looked to fix the external issue.

Was he ready to try something different?

On a bright Monday morning, Todd walked into a run-down coffee shop in a corner of San Francisco that had seen better days. A woman sat in the back corner, her thick brown bangs nearly covering her eyes. She was sipping a pale green drink. A second steaming cup sat off to the side. This must be Cora.

Todd sat down, and they talked about the usual things: the fog, the new exhibit at the San Francisco Museum of Modern Art, the juxtaposition of the city's gentrification with its startling decay. Then her alarm went off.

"Eleven minutes. A new client record," Her voice remained monotone, and he realized how much her flat affect was disarming him. "Let me see if I have this straight. You don't want to talk about the problem. And you're not sure you want to work with me. Sounds like this chat's off to a great start." She leaned forward in her chair. "Todd, how valuable is your time to you?"

"Very," he said, surprised by the question. Did she not know who he was?

"And yet you're still here," she said. She took another sip of her drink. "Do you know how they make good matcha?"

He didn't, so she told him. Good matcha requires time, mastery, and hard work. Things happened in Japan. Then things happened in a coffee shop. Todd was trying to follow the explanation, looking for the metaphor he assumed would apply to him. When she was done, she sat back. She hadn't tied up the story in a bow or made a connection to his potential challenges as a CEO. She looked at him.

"So," she said, "do you want to tell me why you're really here today?"

Todd looked down at his cappuccino. It was cold. He was surprised to realize how much he wanted to tell her about what was really going on at LUNAQ. But then, as he stared at what was left of the foam, marred now by a brown streak of cinnamon still running through it, he decided to do what he always did. He launched into his spiel. Todd spoke of a moderate challenge he was gracefully navigating, given how wise and successful he was. He dropped a couple of big names in for good measure. Along the way, he emphasized how different this challenge was from all the other run-of-the-mill business challenges of the world, including those of other big tech companies, like the one Cora had worked at. Nobody had ever seen something like this. Only he could really understand it.

As he heard himself gloss over his many pain points with a rose-colored paintbrush, he felt better. Maybe sharing his problems, without sharing too much, was all he needed.

Cora listened. Then she said simply, "Todd, I'm going to be honest. I don't think you have a tech company problem, or a start-up problem, or a high-growth problem. I think what you have is a YOU problem. And I think I know how to fix it."

Any warm thoughts he had started to have evaporated in an instant. Who did she think she was, anyway? Had she built a business worth several billion dollars? He looked outside.

"How about that fog?"

Her eyes were on him when her alarm went off again. "It's time for me to go," she said.

"Another client?"

"Nope. The dirt's calling. My brain's got some ideas." He raised an eyebrow. "Gardening, hands in dirt, mind adrift. The default mode network. We'll talk about it if we ever see each other again. Since that seems unlikely, I'd recommend Google."

With that, she was gone.

CHAPTER 6

The chat with Cora wasn't sitting right with Todd, and he told his assistant, Barbara, to gracefully bow him out of the dinner he was supposed to attend that night. He didn't feel up to it. Plus, he hadn't seen much of his family lately.

By the time he got home, they were already seated at the kitchen table and were about to cut into some lasagna. One of his preteen sons looked up at him, blankly. "Mom, I think you forgot to set the alarm."

"We definitely have an intruder," the other son said. They were twins. Identical.

"Have you been fired?" his wife said, suspiciously.

"No…" Todd trailed off. "I just wanted to eat at home for a change."

The three of them exchanged a look and then begrudgingly scooted over to make a place for Todd. Their cell phones were in a basket in the middle of the table, something his wife did to get his kids to talk at dinner. She'd read about it in a book.

As Todd sat down, his phone dinged with a new text. It was from Barbara. Someone was mad he wasn't at the dinner.

"Let me just respond to this real quick," Todd said.

One of the twins yanked the phone right out of his hand. "Nobody is better than the basket."

After a slow start, Todd talked with his kids for fifteen minutes, which made him feel good. One son had a big part in a school play, and Todd heard all about a work of Shakespeare he'd never read. The plot, which was insane, sounded like something that could take place today—not in the 1500s. Todd told his son he would read it first so he could get the most out of the performance. And he would. He was learning. His other son mentioned an expert in artificial intelligence who had given a talk in his robotics class at school, and Todd laughed, sharing his own wisdom. The hot trends will come and go, and artificial intelligence was just such an example. He went on and on. Whatever you do, don't take it too seriously. He was teaching. Learning and teaching. Dad stuff. Todd liked being a father. And they were good kids.

When they went upstairs, Todd was alone with his wife, who hadn't said much at all during dinner.

Mira didn't mince words: "What's going on?"

"What do you mean?"

"Canceling a work dinner? Going to San Diego to sing karaoke? You've been weird ever since you got back from Dubai. I've been patient over the past year as you've basically disappeared from family life entirely, but this feels different. Is there something going on I should know about?"

Todd's phone dinged twice with two more text messages, and he looked longingly at the basket.

"It's not going to save you now," she said.

And that was when Todd let it all out. He started at the

beginning and went to the end. By the time it was over, he felt calmer than he had in ages. Mira reached for his hand.

"Although I'm glad you're not having an affair with a traveling karaoke singer, I'm going to be blunt. You're in some real trouble. And not just at LUNAQ. You need help."

"I know," he said. "I just don't know where to find it."

"What do you mean? Didn't you have coffee with her today?"

"Cora? The matcha? The dirt? I couldn't even understand what we were talking about half the time. I'm not going to waste my time with her again."

"Look, you say you trust Ray. And Ray says she's one of the best. Why not try it? It's the trust chain." Todd's wife loved the trust chain, something her mother had taught her during her childhood in South America. As his wife explained it, when you weren't sure who to put your faith in, your best bet was to trust the people who the people you trusted, trusted. Todd had to admit that the trust chain usually did work. "It's not like you have many other options," she added.

But she's wrong, he thought. He did have other options. Most saliently, he could keep doing what he'd been doing. Ray had explained it to him. Successful people did it all the time. But was that what he wanted? What if this crisis was just the beginning? What if his luck at LUNAQ had run out? And what if he didn't have what it took to meet the new challenges head-on?

Mira interrupted his thoughts.

"I know what you're thinking about," she said. "And it's LUNAQ. So, I'll say this one more time in case you weren't listening. This isn't just about LUNAQ anymore, Todd," she looked at him intently. "Our family is not going to wait forever for you to care about us."

CHAPTER 7

The next morning, Todd called Cora. By the fourth ring, right before he thought it was going to voicemail but right after he remembered millennials like Cora didn't even have voicemail anymore, she picked up.

"Hi, Todd," she said flatly. *Raybot was right,* Todd thought. She really did sound like a robot. An out of breath one today. "Hang on one second, I need to wash my hands."

"Back in the dirt?" he said.

Now she was confused. "Oh. No, no. This is clay. It's much more stubborn."

"You make pots, too?" he said.

"Actually, I make miniature statues of all my clients." Todd drew in a breath. "That's a joke," she said. He let out an audible sigh of relief. Then, despite himself, he began to chuckle. She continued, "Yes, pots, although I wouldn't call them that yet. I'm a beginner, so they're mostly just lumps at this stage."

Todd couldn't care less about Cora's clay, so he surprised himself with his next question. "You really do a lot of…stuff," he said. "Why?"

"That's a story for another day," she said. "But what can I do for you this morning?"

"I'm calling," Todd said, reciting what he'd prepared to say, "because I am committed to making changes in my life, and I would like you to be my executive coach to help me do so."

There was a pause. And then Cora asked, "Todd, have you been kidnapped?"

"What?" Todd said.

"I ask because it sounds like you're reading a ransom note. The tone of voice. The word choice. The lack of fluidity of speech. Did someone put a gun to your head and force you to do this?"

Todd was startled. "No…" he stumbled. "I mean, no! Why would I be calling if I didn't want to?"

"People do all sorts of things for all sorts of reasons," Cora said. "Look," she continued, "I'm busy. You're busy. Let's not waste each other's time, okay? Coaching only works if someone wants to change and wants to put in the work to do so."

Now Todd was scrambling. "Wait, wait! Look, I know I haven't come across as very…*compliant*…but I need this." As an afterthought, he added, "And I want this."

There was another pause on the line. Todd was about to start groveling when Cora spoke.

"You're really in it?" she said.

As soon as he heard the doubt in her voice, he jumped in with a firm tone he hoped marshaled the requisite conviction. "I'm in it," he said.

"Okay," she said. "Then let's do this."

Cora walked him through some of the tenets of her executive coaching practice, emphasizing a few key things. She repeated that she only worked with people who wanted to change. And she, like Ray before her, didn't get paid unless they changed. She determined the success of the behavioral changes not only through her regular individual sessions with Todd, but also through the series of interviews she would conduct with a short list of Todd's closest colleagues, family members, and direct reports. They were called stakeholders. Their feedback at the beginning and the end of her engagement with Todd would be critical.

After Cora had answered some of Todd's questions, he couldn't help but remind her that LUNAQ's problems weren't getting any better. He asked her flat out, "When can we have our first session?"

"We've already had that," she said. "So that means it's time for your first assignment. For next week, I need you to make a list. Pencil on paper, no typing. Your brain connected to your pen. Body memory, haptic needs, process of inquiry. I can send you the research."*

"Okay," Todd said, trying to keep up. "A list of what?"

"A list of everyone you're lying to."

---

* "The Psychology Behind the Pen," Wordwise Blog, Wordsmith, March 25, 2019, http://wordsmith.hk/wordwise-blog/2019/3/22/the-psychology-behind-the-pen; Anne Chemin, "Handwriting vs typing: is the pen still mightier than the keyboard?" *The Guardian*, December 16, 2014, https://www.theguardian.com/science/2014/dec/16/cognitive-benefits-handwriting-decline-typing; William R. Klemm, PhD, "Why Writing by Hand Could Make You Smarter," *Psychology Today*, March 14, 2013, https://www.psychologytoday.com/us/blog/memory-medic/201303/why-writing-hand-could-make-you-smarter; Jane Brunette, "How to Use Writing as a Meditation Practice," *HuffPost*, October 8, 2013, https://www.huffpost.com/entry/writing-meditation_b_4035166.

He stopped himself before he began to protest. “I assume I shouldn’t say I don’t think I am lying?”

“Bingo,” she said. “You’re quick.”

CHAPTER 8

Even though he thought it sounded stupid, Todd resolved to make a good first impression. He spent a good amount of time crafting the long, handwritten list he brought with him to his next meeting with Cora.

"It turns out I'm lying to everyone," he said as he plopped the paper on the table.

Cora asked him to read the list out loud. A few minutes in, after it sounded like he had already listed everyone he knew, including the barista and the pool guy, Todd said, "And all my employees, of course."

That's when Cora spoke up. "How are you lying to all your employees?"

"I'm lying because LUNAQ is in crisis, and they don't know."

"There's a difference between transparency and boundaries. There's a reason we wear clothes in supermarkets, and there's a reason we don't meet our kid's teacher and immediately tell him about all our marital problems. You already know that. Imagine if you thought you might have to downsize later this year at LUNAQ. Would you gather all your employees together six months in advance and tell them you were considering it?"

"Of course not," Todd said. "That would just create chaos."

"Exactly," Cora said. "Look, that was quite a list. But there was someone notably absent. Do you remember what problem I said you had in our first meeting?"

He paused, and the point of the exercise hit him. "Right. Duh. I'm lying to myself."

"And that's what we're going to talk about today," Cora said. "The last time we spoke, you weren't exactly forthcoming about what was really going on at LUNAQ. There's no way I can be helpful if you can't be honest with me about what you're here to work on."

Todd had to admit that Cora was right, and her tactic had been effective.

Over the next twenty minutes, he tried to explain. LUNAQ was a software company that sold large solutions to enterprise clients—the big guys. That's how Todd had started the company, and that's how he was committed to keeping the company.

But the entire industry, the incumbents, and the market had all changed in the past few years. What had started as a slow dip in revenue was now an increasing trough. He was facing headwinds on all sides. The only solution, growth, was proving increasingly elusive. The team was demoralized, the investors were antsy, and the outlook was bleak. Oh, and his only solution? To try and pretend it wasn't happening to keep the lid on. That wasn't working out well at all.

Cora sat back in her chair when he finished. "That's a big story," she said. "How does it feel to tell me about it?"

"It feels…bad?" Todd said. "And also…good? The only other person who knows everything is my wife. Some of the senior leaders know big pieces of it, and I certainly haven't lied to my board members or investors, but I'm the only one who knows the full picture."

"And what is that like? To be the only one?"

"Oh, that's all bad," Todd said.

"Why?"

"Because that means it's all on me. So far, that isn't working. If I already knew how to fix this mess, I would have by now. I was Googling the default mode network you mentioned. It's clear I need more time for my brain to disengage from conscious thought so it can work its way toward some good ideas. More time in the shower, more time walking in silence, more time with my hands in that dirt you spoke of."

"Sounds like a good idea," Cora said. "I think you need that, and I hope you can make a regular practice of doing it now. But you also need something else."

"What's that?" Todd said.

"You need help," Cora said. "And not just from me. You hired a bunch of smart people for a reason. Let them in. Ask them what they think."

CHAPTER 9

It was cold and rainy when Todd stepped out of the office. It had been a week of tough conversations, and he needed a breather: a coffee, a walk, some time to think. Just when he got in line at his favorite coffee shop, his phone rang. Ray de Luca's name flashed on the screen.

"Ray?" Todd said, picking up. "How's it going?"

"Great! In fact, Raybot and I were just thinking about you." Todd could hear the robot muttering in the background. "Also," Ray said, "I thought it was a good time to check in. There was something I forgot to mention the last time we talked."

"Oh?"

"Even though I'm free-range, I like to call up the clients my mentees are coaching every so often to see if I can be of any help. To spread my own fairy dust, as it were."

In the background, Raybot spoke up, "More like coal dust!" Ray clapped back at the robot. Todd ordered a flat white from his regular barista while the Rays hashed it out.

The bickering now over, Ray was back. "So, how are things?"

"I've got to be honest," Todd said, "it's been rough."

He explained that LUNAQ's quarterly board meeting was coming up next week, and he couldn't be more worried. He needed a good idea to get him out of the crisis, and he still didn't have one. To make matters worse, this week had been particularly hellish. Cora had helped him identify the various difficult conversations he needed to have with members of his senior team in advance of the board meeting. As he predicted, they hadn't been fun. In what came as a surprise to him, however, some had also been excruciatingly stupid. Todd had been amazed by the awful ideas that certain members of his C-suite had come up with when he put their feet to the fire. Who were these people he had hired? And what had they done with their brains? Ultimately, he consoled himself with the fact that he could always make them do what he wanted. He was in charge, after all. But next week was a whole different animal.

He kept talking.

"The board is a huge problem. If it weren't for them, I could make the big changes I need, but I need their approval, and they just don't get it. They're stuck in the past. I don't even think they know we're in a recession. Even the director of the board is in his own head too much. Sure, he's the best VC in the valley, but it's been years since he backed the software behemoth that powered practically every tech company in the land. LUNAQ is different! They just don't have my mindset, and it's bringing me down. I mean, if I had my way, I'd—"

"Todd, let me stop you there," Ray said. He paused. "I've got a question. You're a CEO, right?"

"Right," Todd said. He wondered where this was going.

"And you're not just any CEO. You're a big one. You've got one of the hottest companies in Silicon Valley. You're on the cover of all the magazines. You're invited to the fancy things. You've raised nearly a billion dollars, and you still own what, 15 percent, maybe 20 percent of your company? You're a pretty big deal, right?"

"I guess that's fair to say," Todd said. This coaching was starting to make him feel a little better after all.

"You know who's a bigger deal than you?" Ray said.

"Who?" Todd said.

"Your board of directors," Ray said. "The sooner you learn that, the better."

Todd felt like he'd been punched in the face. He looked down at what was left of his flat white. How the hell was he supposed to respond to that?

Ray didn't seem to notice the silence. "Well, I've got to go," he said brightly. "Karaoke? Soon?"

In the background, Todd could hear Raybot loud and clear this time. "I told you, Todd. Coal dust!"

CHAPTER 10

A few days later, Todd was on the phone with Cora. They weren't at the coffee shop this week, but she'd already mentioned the turmeric and cacao in her mug.

"It has the consistency of mulch," she said with more animation in her voice than Todd was used to.

"Mulch?" Todd said. Not for the first time, he thought Raybot had been right when it came to Cora. Right about a lot of things, actually. Todd brought the conversation back to work. "I did the thing we talked about. I asked for ideas."

"And how'd that go?" Cora said.

"I got some really bad ones!" Todd said. He held himself back from saying what a terrible suggestion it had been.

"Good," Cora said. "Did you know that some of the best ideas can look like the very worst ideas at first?"

"What do you mean?" Todd said.

"You're the founder; you already know this. Driving people around in your own car for money even though you're not a taxi driver? Telling people on the Internet what you ate for breakfast? Those bad ideas certainly turned out well," Cora said.

"True," Todd said.

"But that can only happen if you have the secret ingredient," Cora said.

"Which is?" Todd said.

"Time. A bad idea, with enough time, can sometimes become a great idea. People romanticize this idea that Einstein was in the bath one day and—poof—the theory of relativity! But does anyone ever ask how many baths of bad ideas he took? The development of good ideas is a process, and we need to allow time for them to emerge."

"Unfortunately, I don't have much of that," Todd said. "I guess I better make the best of it and find more people to ask about what I should do." He didn't mention that he was starting to doubt if he should bother to include Cora on that list.

"Hold on there," Cora said. "This isn't about crowdsourcing your life. I'm not suggesting you ask people who don't know what they're talking about. Would you take advice on fixing your car from someone who wasn't a mechanic?"

"No," Todd said.

"So, have you been asking anyone about LUNAQ who really isn't in the best position to provide advice?"

"I'm not sure what you mean by that," Todd said. "The best position."

"Well, everyone has their own expertise, but everyone also has their own priorities. You wouldn't ask someone who's not a mechanic to fix your car, but you also might not ask a brand-new mechanic who doesn't have as much experience. If you needed your car fixed immediately, you also might not first ask a mechanic who's got twenty cars ahead of you. And, if you want your car fixed as cheaply as possible, you might not go to Beverly Hills and look for a mechanic there. Whenever you are seeking advice, you've got to consider the perspective and goals of the person giving it and the amount of information they really have. Remember, you are the only person in your shoes." Todd could understand that. "So, have you talked to anyone who doesn't share your goals or doesn't have a full enough picture of the situation to give sound advice?" Cora said.

Todd thought about it. Most of his conversations had been with the C-suite members he and Cora had identified beforehand, but not all of them. In his desperation for an answer, he'd taken it upon himself to call in a few others as well. There had been some real misses. His treasurer, a genius with numbers, had gotten way too stuck on them and couldn't see anything else. Todd didn't need somebody else to bemoan how bad the figures were—he needed someone who could help him brainstorm solutions despite them! His head of engineering, another fantastic professional, couldn't get past the fact that he might have to lay off team members. Todd was obviously very concerned about that as well, but as CEO, he knew it could not be the primary issue when it came to saving the company.

There had also been some good conversations. His chief marketing officer had brought up some points he hadn't thought about. His chief financial officer had suggested something that sounded crazy, but, in retrospect, might be worth considering. And his chief revenue officer had really given him pause. In a good way. Although she hadn't provided any specific suggestions for what to do, she did seem to fully understand the real issues at hand in a way that few others did.

It was all a lot to think about.

"I take your point," Todd said reluctantly. "And I need to think on it more." Knowing Cora's mulch was likely a congealed mass at the bottom of her stainless-steel tumbler by now, he begged off. "Give me a few days. I might be closer to a good idea than I realized."

CHAPTER 11

When he got in the car to drive home that night, Todd decided not to turn on a podcast. Cora had suggested he spend some more time in silence. She called it one of her "tools." It was strange not to listen to anything as he drove, since he was always taking in information. It felt nice to let his mind roam.

He got off at his regular freeway exit and was waiting at a stoplight when he saw a big wooden sign he hadn't noticed before.

Free mulch! And a labyrinth!

It was the second time he'd thought of that word today, thanks to Cora's drink. Come to think of it, his wife also mentioned it from time to time. She had a small compost pile in their yard. What had she said about it again? To be honest, he had never paid much attention. He made a split-second decision to follow the arrow on the sign. He certainly wasn't winning any awards for best husband these days. Maybe he could bring home some mulch for his wife? And maybe she'd like it?

After a few turns, he found himself on a winding road tucked into the hills just a few minutes from his own house.

All the houses were set back far from the street, and when the sign appeared again, he turned onto a long driveway. At the end, stood a huge house set on the manicured grounds typical of his upscale suburb on the San Francisco Peninsula. But then he looked closer. A large, derelict shed with a jumble of compost bins in front of it sat off to one side of the oversized lot. Next to it was an old orange van, and beyond it a carefully tended row of fruit trees. A young man in overalls had lifted the lid on one of the bins and was poking at whatever was inside. Todd got out of his car and approached. As he did so, he got a better look at the strange rows of untamed hedges that rose behind the structure.

"What is this place?" Todd said in greeting.

"Hi!" the young man said. "Do you need mulch?"

"I do," Todd said.

"Cool! A customer!" The young man smiled. "While I get it ready, go try the labyrinth."

"Where does it go?" Todd said.

This time, the young man laughed. "To the middle, of course."

"And then what?"

"Then you come back out again!"

Todd didn't get it, but he figured he might as well try it out. It wasn't large, and it didn't have any of the tricky false paths Todd expected. It took less than ten minutes to weave his way into the center, where there was a tiny bird bath next to a bench cut out of an old log. He sat down for a moment and looked around. Over the hedge, he could see the big mansion next to him and a row of fruit trees. Not sure what else to do, he walked back out. The young man was at the compost bins; he was shoveling mulch into a bag.

"I don't really know if I did it right," Todd said.

"Did you get to the middle?" the young man said.

"Yeah," Todd said.

"Then I think you did it right."

"What's the deal with this place?" Todd said. "It doesn't really look like a farm."

"Nah, it's my mom's place. She's a venture capitalist."

"I see," Todd said. "And you are...?"

"Right now, I'm a nothing," the young man said. "I was a college student. Computer engineering."

"And then what?"

"Everything got too noisy."

"What do you mean?"

The young man put the shovel down. "Ever since I was a kid, I always thought I wanted to be a computer engineer. But then, once I was really doing it, I started having new thoughts. Like, what if I really want to be an actor? Or a biologist? I had too many different ideas banging around in my head. And then I was here one weekend, and I found a book in my mom's library. It said that if you're trying to climb the ladder of success, you better be darn sure you're climbing the right ladder. That got me thinking. What ladder was I on anyway? And was it the right one?"

"Did you figure it out?" Todd said.

"No," the young man said. "That's why I'm taking some time off. I need to create some space for time to happen." The young man gestured vaguely around him. "That was also from the book."

"And you don't ever worry about falling behind?"

"How could I be behind if I don't know where I'm trying to go?"

"I guess I've never thought of it like that," Todd said. "So now you're...composting?"

"I like to think I'm out here listening. Listening to the mulch."

There was that word again. "Which means?"

"Well, there's a lot to learn from compost. Good compost is like a great salad. An earth salad. You need a little of this, a little of that. Food scraps. Coffee grounds. Eggshells. You can't have too much of one thing. It's more art than science. So that's why you've got to listen to the mulch."

"And how do you do that?"

"It'll tell you if you're quiet enough."

"It will?"

"Oh, sure. Too wet, too stinky, too dry. So, I guess that's what I'm doing. I'm trying to listen."

"Seems like a good thing to do," Todd said.

The young man had finished and plopped the big bag into the open trunk of Todd's car.

"Well, looks like you're set. The next time you need some more, feel free to stop by. I might still be here."

Todd smiled. "Or you might not."

The kid smiled. "Fair point."

"Hey," Todd said. "Who wrote the book?"

The kid looked up to the sky, trying to remember. "I forget his name, but I'd remember the author's face anyway. Fluffy white curly hair. Purple shirt. Huge smile."

Todd had figured as much.

By the time he turned off the driveway, he already knew what he had to do next when it came to LUNAQ.

CHAPTER 12

"So, how are you feeling about Monday's meeting?" Cora said.

Todd was in his home office this time, talking to Cora on the phone as she walked around the city trying to get in her 9,711 steps.

"Not 10,000?" Todd asked.

"Too predictable," she said.

It was the Saturday morning before Monday's big board meeting, and Todd was telling her how great he was feeling. So great that he'd meant to cancel on her. Somehow, he'd found himself calling instead. But it would be quick, he decided. "I know exactly what I'm going to do to position the content the team will be presenting. I've got it all planned out. And I'm going to spend the weekend putting it in place."

"That's great," Cora said. "Tell me about it."

"Well, it all started when Ray threw his coal dust on me and said I wasn't as big of a deal as I thought I was. I told you about that. And then you told me Einstein took a lot of bad baths, and that got my mind going. When I met the kid with the mulch, it all came together."

"I'm not sure I'm following," Cora said.

"At the end of the day," Todd said, "it's all about listening. I know I must do it better, but I also need to be judicious about who I'm listening to."

"So, you're listening to the kid with the mulch?" Cora said.

"Yes," Todd said.

"Perfect," Cora said in her usual monotone. Todd knew by now she wasn't being sarcastic. "Sounds like you figured out that there's a difference between crowd-sourcing your life from people who aren't authorized to speak on your situation and looking for moments of inspiration. In this case, you didn't ask the kid with the mulch exactly how to solve the LUNAQ problem, which would not have been advisable for a variety of reasons, including some the Securities and Exchange Commission would likely deem illegal. But you did keep your ears open for inspiration in unusual places. I love it. So, tell me how you've decided to approach the presentation."

"It's okay," Todd said. "I'm actually good."

"Good?"

"Yeah, I don't need feedback on this one. I'm the one wearing my shoes, like you said. I've got it."

"Okay," Cora said after a pause. "But remember, I'm just a call away."

"Sure," Todd said quickly before hanging up the phone.

He had a lot of work to do.

CHAPTER 13

Todd spent all weekend preparing for the big board meeting. Although he typically would have had his team preview the final versions of his slide deck, that wouldn't work this time. Not even his most senior leaders had all the information he had. This was one of the most sensitive board presentations of his life, and the hard stuff could only come from him. Thankfully, he was eager to try his hand at some of the things he'd learned from the storytelling masters at TED to frame the difficult discussion. As he'd said to Cora, he didn't need her input on it either.

He had it all under control.

The upscale hotel conference area where they usually held their quarterly meetings was pristine; the board members were watching him with anticipation. He was twenty minutes into the presentation on Monday morning when he stopped to take a question from one of his board members who was seated at a long table. Todd was taking longer than he'd planned to get through his deck, and he was only on the fifth slide. A pixelated worm stared out from the screen at the audience.

LUNAQ's lead venture capital investor spoke. "So, the mulch kid said to listen to the salad?"

"Exactly," Todd said, glad to see they were getting it. "The earth salad."

"Remind me what that was again?" the CFO of a telecom company at the end of the table said.

"We're the salad," another board member said. "The coffee grounds, the broken eggs, the food scraps—"

"So, Todd should listen to us?" the telecom executive said.

"Yes!" Todd said, pointing at her this time. "You've got it!"

The board members exchanged confused glances. It was the lead investor again who was the first to say it. "I like hearing myself speak as much as the next person, but what exactly are you supposed to listen to us about?"

"Oh!" Todd had completely forgotten. After slide three—or was it slide four?—he'd meant to pause the deck and lay out the crisis at LUNAQ. There had been a good transition...had it been a joke? About the mulch? He couldn't remember anymore, but he knew it had been funny when he'd practiced it in front of the bathroom mirror. Flustered, he ran to flip the lights back on.

Back at the head of the table, he began to speak. "The first part was a metaphor before I explained what I really have to tell you—"

"We get it," the lead investor said, who didn't. "Just tell us what's going on."

"Please," the telecom executive said.

The other board members nodded.

So, Todd laid it out. When he was done speaking, there was a long silence. And then the complaints began.

But last quarter, things didn't seem as bad—

How could you just spring this on us—

I don't understand why we weren't given more information beforehand to prepare for what is arguably the most important board meeting we've had—

In thirty years of being on boards, I've never had—

Why did we have to sit through twenty minutes of gardening instruction—

Over the next hour, Todd did his best to field questions about the mess at LUNAQ. But the frustration at this unwelcome company update was palpable. The members of his own senior team in the room looked equally stunned. He could see now he had gone about everything all wrong—starting with the way he'd tried to diminish the board's concerns when things started to go badly, all the way up until the moment he had decided to do the presentation on his own, surprising everyone with the weight of everything they didn't know.

There was something else. Something developing inside him, gnawing at him—he could feel it. Todd had spent a lot of time winning over the years. Sure, there had been problems, even big ones—bad launches, hires that hadn't worked out, difficult capital raises—but he'd never, ever felt what he was feeling now. And whatever this was, he never, ever wanted to feel it again. Lost in his thoughts, he drifted over toward the window. It had been raining earlier this morning, but now he could see a big storm coming in. Somewhere, Todd could hear the board still talking.

His lead investor was trying to get his attention. "Todd? Are you there? Earth to Todd! Come back to Planet Earth—"

"Oh God, not the salad again," the telecom executive said.

Another board member was chiming in now. "Nothing,

nothing will ever top that worm slide...it was so—"

"Pixelated?" another said.

Now, someone was tapping his shoulder.

"Todd?" It was Heidi, his chief revenue officer. Along with LUNAQ's COO, she was the most important executive in the business. Although lately, Todd had to agree with the COO that Heidi had been getting a little too involved in things that didn't concern her. "I'm calling a ten-minute break."

By the time he got back to the room, everyone was in their seats again, fresh coffees and waters all around. Andrew, the COO, led Todd to a seat. Wasn't this where Heidi was sitting? He now realized she was standing at the front of the room. But her part of the presentation wasn't supposed to start until he finished. He started to protest, but Andrew gave him a sharp look. "Heidi's taking it from here," he said. What was going on? Andrew *hated* Heidi. Andrew practically shoved Todd into his chair. "We're pivoting."

Over the next fifteen minutes, Heidi tried to reestablish a measure of trust with the board members. She took responsibility on behalf of Todd and the other members of the C-suite for diminishing the concerns they'd had about flagging topline revenue growth, she shared how important it was for them to be transparent about their concerns and to tap into their wisdom, and she listened. Todd had to give it to her; she was taking a lot of responsibility for someone who didn't know the entire picture. That's when she dimmed the lights and pulled up a slide.

"In the spirit of transparency," she said, "I want to share with you the idea for one path I've been considering that could ameliorate some of our problems." Heidi pointed to the graph on the screen. It showed the stark reality of what Todd had been explaining. The board members leaned forward in their chairs. It was good for the board to see it laid out like this, and Todd couldn't help but think that this was how he should have started his own presentation. Not with the worm. Heidi clicked to a new slide. He saw some board members nodding. She kept clicking.

Ten minutes later, she was deep into the discussion.

"We used to rely on always getting the biggest clients, but over the past five years, many new competitors have come into the market. We're seen as an established player now, which can sometimes work against us. After all, it's usually the hottest start-ups that get the shiniest deals. Plus, start-ups have a natural growth cycle. Some of the small clients that the new entrants signed on a few years ago have grown up. A few of them are now behemoths. The new entrants are now firmly our competition. All this to say, we have fewer big players on our books than we did five years ago. And our projections are shrinking."

"So, what do we do?" a board member said.

"We go down-market," Heidi said.

"Down-market?" Todd couldn't help but raise his voice.

She pulled up another slide where she'd laid out her plan. As she began to talk through it, beads of sweat popped up at Todd's temples. He looked around him. The telecom executive was nodding. His lead venture capital investor had leaned forward in his chair. Todd tapped his finger against his leg anxiously. He pushed his chair back and put his arms behind his head, bumping the shoulder of the telecom executive next to him.

"Sorry," he said to her under his breath. Finally, he stood

up, knocking over the glass of water that was sitting on the table in front of him, spilling water onto the notes of the board member to his left.

"Sorry," he said again. He went to the back of the room to grab a napkin. He came back to the table and started wiping up the mess, but then he realized he needed a second napkin. He came back. He kept wiping, but as he did so, he knocked his own phone to the floor. He was making a scene now. Heidi was still talking, louder, trying to keep the attention of the board and, more slowly, looking at him, trying to figure out what was going on.

"Do we need to take another quick break?" Heidi said.

He shot her a glance. No, he didn't need a break. He'd just had one. He wasn't a child! And who did she think she was, anyway? What he needed was to think. He had started LUNAQ with one vision: To be the best enterprise software solution provider in the market, they would focus on the massive, big-name vendors and eschew the little guys. It was the one way to win, and he stood behind it. He had gotten a large amount of funding to give him the time to prove the strategy, and it had worked. Their bread and butter had always been the huge, long-term contracts. Sure, they took a while to close, but once you got them, you could rely on them for years. Going down-market was unthinkable. At some point, he realized the table was dry and that he was speaking out loud.

"We don't even *have* a down-market solution," he heard himself saying. "And even if we did, how could we execute on it while also reducing head count, which we know we need to do to cut our burn? The basic tenet of our industry is that one big client often requires just as much effort to close as a smaller one. The idea will never work. We would need significantly more staff in sales and support."

"Not if we use an AI solution," Heidi said. She clicked to a new slide.

Todd couldn't believe what he'd just heard. His head began to spin, a mix of rage and fear overtaking him, the sweat now beginning to drip down his face. His heart was thumping out of his chest, and he needed to get out of this place, away from these horrible ideas and all these stupid people who weren't smart enough to see things the way he saw them. Why couldn't they just be more like him? He threw the wet napkins down and stepped back from the table, hearing his iPhone crunch under the heel of his boot as he did so.

If this was a coup d'état, then this was one hell of a fall from grace.

PART 2

OPEN TO FEEDBACK

CHAPTER 14

At noon the next day, Todd was in bed and staring at his phone when his wife came into the room.

"You're back in bed?" she said.

"I'm *still* in bed," he said. "I'm not getting out, either."

After opening the curtains and turning on the lights, Mira approached. Pulling the covers off Todd's head, she reached for his phone.

"Give me that," she said.

"Gladly," Todd said. "Now you can respond to them."

"Are there a lot of messages?"

Todd snorted. "The main email chain my lead investor started, which is titled, rather unimaginatively, 'Next Steps,' has twenty-seven responses. Some go on for pages. But nine other one-on-one or small group chains are also live and well, some complementary in their overlap, and some in direct contrast to one another. And that's only on email. In terms of text messages, there are twenty-one."

Mira looked down at the phone in her hand as it dinged.

"Twenty-two," he said.

"And what are you saying to everyone?"

This time, Todd laughed. "Nothing," Todd said. "I am saying absolutely nothing." Mira stared as he fluffed his pillows, one by one, and then propped them up behind him. Reaching for a crisp new detective novel on his bedside table, he cracked the spine. "Let's see which sad sack is going to die today. They never do see it coming!"

He let out another guffaw as Mira closed the door behind her. She could hear his phone, which she'd left on the dresser, ding again. She reached into her pocket and pulled out her own, scrolling quickly to find the number she wanted. She sent a quick text.

Would it be possible to talk today?

CHAPTER 15

Two hours later, Todd still hadn't left his bed. Mira logged onto a videoconference call from her home office. She sat in the waiting room for a minute before Cora's face appeared on the screen. Just as Todd had described, she was sipping from a mug. It was probably warm.

"Thanks for meeting with me," Cora said.

"Thank you for finding the time," Mira said. "I know we were scheduled for later this week but, given everything that's happened in the past twenty-four hours, I wanted to speak today."

"No problem," Cora said. "Why don't I give you an overview of the process as I explained in the email, and then you can catch me up?"

Mira nodded in agreement, and over the next few minutes, Cora explained the nature of their scheduled phone call. As an executive coach, Cora adhered to the process of 360-degree feedback, also known as multi-rater feedback. The process had a long history in organizations, going back to the 1950s. It was a key feature of Stakeholder-Centered Coaching, one of various methodologies that Ray de Luca and Cora were trained in. In

Ray's Stanford PhD program, he had even analyzed the results of the process, with 60,000 working professionals, proving its efficacy. Whenever Cora started with a client, she identified early on the key issues the client wanted to work on. These might come from the client himself, or, when a board member or boss referred a client to Cora, the feedback could come from the referrer. Either way, Cora never worked with clients who weren't internally motivated to make a change.

After establishing key behavioral concerns with the coach, the client would then identify a list of individuals, or "stakeholders," who were affected by the client's ongoing behavior and would have insight into the changes the client wanted to make. This was usually a mix of professional and personal contacts. Cora first involved these stakeholders in the change process by interviewing them at the beginning of the client engagement. Their initial feedback would help direct the plan for her work with the client.

Stakeholders were essential to the process, and their feedback could direct a whole engagement. As an example, a client might come in thinking they had one set of behavioral changes they wanted to make, but early feedback from stakeholders might suggest that those weren't the actual problematic behaviors. Or a client might state an issue they were facing and not know what behaviors were associated with fixing the problem. The initial round of stakeholder interviews could clarify what behavior was aggravating this problem. At the end of the engagement, which usually took six to twelve months, Cora would go back to these same stakeholders to see if there had been positive progress. Cora, like her mentor Ray, only collected a fee if the leader had made positive progress, and there was evidence of behavioral change according to the stakeholders.

Like many clients, Todd had included his spouse as one of his stakeholders, and Cora was eager to learn what she could about Todd's interpretations of the problems he was facing and whether they coincided or conflicted with his wife's perceptions.

When she was finished explaining, Mira spoke up. "I wish for your sake we weren't talking today."

"What do you mean?" Cora said.

"Well, it sounds like you're most interested in the usual behaviors Todd needs to change to be more successful, but most of what I've got to say today has nothing to do with the usual."

"Tell me more," Cora said, leaning in.

Mira then explained everything that had happened since Todd had come home from the board meeting yesterday. The one whiskey, neat. *Todd never drinks.* The takeout pizza, extra breadsticks. *Todd never eats carbs on weekdays.* The three hours watching a replay of a golf tournament. *Todd hates golf.* And then, after the kids had gone upstairs, the opening up about everything that had happened that day. *Todd never has time to talk anymore.*

"And that's before I found him still in bed at noon."

"Is he okay?" Cora said.

"He's great!" Mira said. "Which seems to be the problem. He's still in bed, reading a crime novel and not responding to any of his investors. Although he's been reading every word they've sent."

Cora didn't mention he hadn't responded to her either. "And you say you've never seen him act like this before?"

"Never," Mira said. "Todd's always been so successful. In college, they used to call him The Golden Boy. Later, when he joined the Peace Corps in Kenya, they gave him a nickname—Makena, Kikuyu for 'happy one'—because he was always smiling. By the time we met in graduate school, he still had the golden touch. He could do no wrong. And he always had such a positive attitude about everything!"

Cora listened carefully. "And how would you describe Todd's attitude recently? Is it still very positive?"

Now it was time for Mira to sit back in her chair. "Well, it's nowhere near as upbeat as it used to be." It was true that Todd's general positivity had dropped off in the past year or so, but it was truer that Todd simply hadn't been around for anyone in the family to see what his attitude was like in the first place. She tried to think of some positive things Todd had done in the past few months. "He came home for dinner the other night," she thought of her son Trevor, complaining the next morning that Todd had mansplained artificial intelligence to him. "And he did bring me a bag of...mulch." She didn't mention to Cora that she'd stopped composting the year before. Composting was one of those things that look a lot better on the Internet. "I guess I wouldn't describe him as very positive anymore, no. But I'm also not sure I would be the best person to ask, given that I never see him..." she trailed off, lost in thought.

"Mira, let me ask you a question."

"Sure."

"Has Todd experienced a lot of major challenges or adversity in his life?"

Mira looked up at the ceiling. She drew out her answer. "Not really. I mean, his brother just got divorced, and his parents are aging, of course..." she tried to cast her mind farther back. "When our boys were little, there were a lot of broken bones from sports, and before he became an entrepreneur, he did have one really bad boss. He gets so much of his self-worth from his career that I know that was a hard experience for him, but it didn't go on for too long. And with LUNAQ, there have definitely been some challenges along the way."

"Let's try a different question," Cora said. "Have you ever seen Todd behave like this before?"

"Definitely not!" Mira said.

But as soon as she said it, she realized she was wrong. Her memory flashed back a dozen years. She and Todd had been dating for a while, and she had wanted to get married and have a baby. At the time, Todd had said that he wasn't ready; he was way too young, and he'd wanted to focus on his career for a few more years first. They'd been having the same conversation for months. They'd even gone to a couple's counselor, a guy Mira hated. There was always a scrawny black cat in his office. She'd told the counselor she was allergic, but the cat was always there, scratching up against the couch, looking up at her with those awful yellow eyes.

Mira and Todd had been in a deadlock. Mira had wanted to move forward and build a family, and Todd had wanted to keep things exactly as they were. One day, she'd realized she didn't have to keep waiting. She could have a great life without him: a career, a baby, another husband. She'd packed her bags, and she'd left. She had told him she was done.

It was only after several months apart, after he had apologized, after he had begged for her hand in marriage, that she had learned how bad it had gotten. For two weeks after she'd left their shared apartment, Todd had called in sick to work, staying in bed and thumbing through newspapers all day. For the two months after that, he hadn't spoken to anyone in his life who hadn't already happened to be sitting next to him in his office. He had ignored calls from his family, he had turned down social invitations from his friends. It was only after his life was on track again—after things were good with Mira, after he had decided he was ready for marriage—that he had let everyone back in. It was only then that he had been able to face the world.

On the screen, Cora was nodding along to Mira's story.

"From what you've described, it sounds like Todd has had a remarkably positive attitude toward what has been a remarkably positive life," Cora said flatly in her distinctive monotone. "The problem now is that things aren't so positive. He's trapped inside a dumpster, and it's on fire, and he can't find his way out."

The unsettling image burned across Mira's mind. It wasn't subtle. "That sounds...bad," she said. "How worried should I be?"

"I'm not going to lie to you, Mira. The next few months will be touch and go. But in the long run? This could be a very good thing."

"It could?"

"Absolutely," Cora said. "What's the best thing that can happen to a leader who's always winning? A crisis. There's nothing like a good, raging dumpster fire to transform a leader for the better."

Mira thought about that. It was a saying, that was for sure.

CHAPTER 16

Cora was in back-to-back meetings over the next few days. After ten text messages to Todd, she still hadn't heard from him. But even if he wasn't talking to her, everyone else in his life was. Cora always reviewed her notes before each call with a client's stakeholder. In her initial discussions with Todd, he had made it clear he'd needed help navigating a crisis. Todd had also provided insight into a host of potential behaviors that were causing problems.

"I'm definitely a perfectionist," he had said back at their first coffee shop meeting. "And everyone says I hold people to a very high standard. And that I can be too hard on them. Wait, are those the same things?"

"It depends," Cora had said. "They can be."

"Also, I'm impatient," he had said. Cora had nodded. "But only when people are moving slowly. Which is why I don't hire slow people. And I don't mince words. I know that can rub people the wrong way, but I like to say it how I see it. Which is why I hire people who talk like me."

"Got it," Cora had said.

As Cora began to do her interviews with Todd's stakeholders, she found that some of the feedback she received coincided with what Todd had said. And some of it didn't. The telecom executive, who turned out to be hungry for change at LUNAQ, cited Todd's hesitance as the real blocker. The lead investor agreed, saying that the board was not only eager to look at new ideas, but often brought in their own. He cited a list of specific suggestions the board had proactively made that Todd had shot down. The board member had even gone so far as to say that Todd always had trouble with an idea when he wasn't the one coming up with it. Another board member agreed that it was Todd, alongside some of the C-suite members, who were most resistant to change. This pattern interested Cora, and she pressed further in her interviews to better understand the perceptions of Todd's stakeholders.

And then there was something else. A few of the stakeholders Todd had suggested didn't seem to have much feedback *at all*. The CFO, for one, had very little to say. The general counsel didn't share much either. Cora had seen a lot of C-suite dynamics in her time as an executive coach, and this was an interesting one. Next up was her call with LUNAQ's COO.

How would that go?

CHAPTER 17

Andrew, the COO, was five minutes late for the call.

Sorry, he texted Cora. *I'll be right there.*

No worries, Cora wrote back.

Once he was logged on, and they had exchanged pleasantries, Cora reviewed the dynamics and purpose of the feedback sessions she was conducting. Then she shifted gears, starting where she always started.

"Andrew, catch me up."

He laughed nervously. "Well, a lot's been going on this week!"

"That's what I hear," Cora said.

"Yeah," Andrew cleared his throat. "It's been...a lot..." His voice trailed off as his eyes shifted offscreen. Cora let the silence hang there until his eyes came back to hers.

"Do you have something to say?" Cora said.

"No..." Andrew said.

"Okay," Cora said. "Because it sounded like you might."

Andrew sat back in his seat. "Look," he said. "I understand this whole coaching thing is what Todd wanted, and I always respect Todd's decisions, but in my experience, I haven't found it to be too effective." He shrugged his shoulders. "And then it turns out it's not just regular coaching; it's this whole thing that involves other people in someone else's coaching...well, it just doesn't seem like the best use of my time this week, given everything that is happening."

"Thanks for sharing that," Cora said. "It's true that not all coaches use 360-feedback, including Todd's past executive coaches, and it sounds like that was your experience as well. Do you think Todd would be surprised by your take on coaching?"

"No," Andrew said. "He knows I didn't have a good experience when I tried it."

"So, why do you think Todd wanted me to talk to you?"

"Honestly, I'm not sure," Andrew said. "I don't even have anything to say, really. Todd and I get along great. In fact, we're old friends, from before LUNAQ. We always see eye to eye. I'm his right-hand man, and I do what he wants done. As he says, I know what he's thinking even before he thinks it!"

"Interesting," Cora said. "So, let's say I were to give you this hour of your life back. What would you do with that time?"

"Well...I guess I'd be on the phone with Todd."

"You would?"

"Yeah."

"So, you and Todd are speaking right now?"

"Well, we're texting," Andrew said. "I mean, I don't agree with everything he's doing right now, but I agree with most of it. I also think everyone else is being too hard on him. You know how boards can be. I'm trying to broker peace between him and the investors."

"And how are you trying to do that?"

"I'm trying to get them to see his perspective. Like I said, he and I think so similarly. I'm pretty sure if I can just calm everybody down, then I can show them what he really meant to say."

"Has it been working?"

If Andrew had thought he was on a roll, now he was stuck. "It could be better. You know..." He didn't elaborate.

Cora nodded. "By the way, have you ever been in this position before?"

Andrew thought about it. "I mean, we've been working together for a decade now. Todd's never been great at conflict, and it's something I don't mind, so it seems like a natural division of labor, you know? When he missteps with an investor or a big client, I can come in and make things better." The nervous laughter that followed sounded different this time.

Cora nodded her head. "That must be great for Todd," she said.

Now it was Andrew's turn to nod. As he did so, she saw a flash of recognition in his eyes. "Yeah...it must be."

CHAPTER 18

Heidi, LUNAQ's chief revenue officer, was already on the videoconference when Cora logged in.

"Finally!" she said. "I feel like I've been waiting all week for this!"

"That's good to hear," Cora said. "I'm not always wanted by all my clients' stakeholders."

After Cora got Heidi up to speed on the purpose of this first conversation, Cora said what she usually did.

"Catch me up."

And Heidi did. Starting a few months back, she painted the picture of LUNAQ's crisis through her eyes, all the way up to the moment that Todd had stormed out of the board meeting.

"Let me ask you a question," Cora said. "How did you come to work at LUNAQ?"

"Oh, that's a funny story. I was working at one of LUNAQ's competitors—well, that was what we called ourselves, but we were much smaller—and LUNAQ started sniffing around, interested in an acquisition. I was the chief revenue officer there as well, and I was tasked with some of the presentations. Usually, it was the CEO who was leading the conference calls, but at times I'd take over on certain points.

"One day there was a specific user metric Todd was really digging in on that was affecting our sales. What's important to the story is that the metric wasn't great—it was only average—which obviously wasn't a good thing for our company's chance at acquisition. That said, Todd had developed this whole story in his head about *why* it was occurring. But he was wrong about it, which meant he was also going to be wrong about how to fix it. He wouldn't listen at first, and so I had to get strong with him. He kept cutting in while I was trying to explain. I was polite, but I told him to please not interrupt me. He listened, and then, finally, he understood. He didn't end up acquiring the company, but he did end up poaching me!"

"Do you and Todd still maintain that type of rapport in your working relationship?" Cora asked.

"I thought we did. But as I've been taking on more responsibility lately, I've noticed a shift. I wouldn't say he doesn't support me, but..." Heidi trailed off. "And after Monday's board meeting, I don't know what to think anymore."

"So what *are* you thinking?" Cora said.

"Honestly? That I'm fired. And that the company is going down. And that Todd bought a tiny house on wheels and is off finding himself in the desert."

"So, you haven't heard from him either?"

"Nope," Heidi said. "But I know he's reading my messages."

"How do you know that?"

"There was an emoji. Two, really. The first looked like a pile of...you know what. But then there was a flower. I know he was talking a lot about compost at the board meeting. Maybe he thought he was sending me a dirt emoji...with the flower growing in it? A few minutes after he sent it, he deleted it. The poop one, not the flower."

Cora tried not to visibly grimace. "Let's go back to what you're thinking right now about the future of LUNAQ. If you had to guess, would you say the other senior leaders are thinking the same as you?"

"I'd say everyone who was in that board room is thinking what I'm thinking." She paused. "Except for his Yes Men, of course."

"His Yes Men?"

"Yeah, you know...Andrew, Celeste, Tina: the COO, the CFO, the general counsel. Oh, and Phil, another board member, though I don't know much about him."

As a coach for senior leaders, and as an executive at a hot tech company before that, Cora was all too familiar with the concept of Yes Men. The more successful a leader became, the more Yes Men seemed to magically sprout up around him. Yes Men were other people—senior leaders, employees, friends—who never challenged the leader on anything; their job was to say "yes," no matter what. Sometimes they did it to directly curry favor, but a lot of the time it was just the pattern of relationship that had developed. The higher a leader rose, the less real dissent they heard.

She remembered a story Ray once told her about a CEO who once grumbled about the cost of an extravagant company offsite; he joked that they should just hold next year's offsite in the parking lot to save money. The next year? It was in the parking lot. And although it was natural in many ways that this dynamic occurred—after all, people want to be around successful people—it was something that good leaders worked to fight against. This was the first time she was hearing about this dynamic at LUNAQ.

"Todd has really, really good ideas most of the time," Heidi was saying. "And Todd is really, really good at his job most of the time. That's what has made LUNAQ such a success. But this is not such a time. And Todd can't see it."

CHAPTER 19

After Cora's feedback session with Heidi, the last of her interviews with Todd's stakeholders, she sat back in her chair. She had been a coach for years now, and she'd always been grateful for the power of 360-degree feedback to get a full picture of what her clients were facing. This experience with Todd was no different. Cora had learned a lot about her client. But something else felt different this time, and it was starting to worry her. What was it?

It was midafternoon in San Francisco, and a weak sun was peeking through the clouds outside her window. Cora pushed her notes aside and stood up from her desk. It was time for a walk. Two hours later, she trudged back up the steps of her house. Physically, she felt tired. Mentally, she felt exhausted. On the walk, she had tried to disconnect and let her mind do its thing. Instead, she'd kept ruminating on what exactly was bothering her about the Todd situation and how she could fix it. Unsurprisingly, the mental grinding had led to no new insights, aside from the fact that her new trail runners were half a size too small. Don't buy shoes on the Internet. Lesson learned.

On Saturday, she went to her ceramics studio. She had a monthly pass, which let her drop in on classes and come in to work on her own. Although she was grateful for the instruction from the classes—she was a newbie, after all—she preferred the solo work. Art was a wonderful way to stop her brain from thinking so hard, and she found that the combination of art plus silence often let something brilliant emerge.

For more than an hour, Cora tried to throw a pot. She cut a big slab of clay with the straight wire, she kneaded out the air bubbles with the heels of her hands, and she took the blob to the wheel. Again and again, she tried to turn it into something presentable. Again and again, she failed. At least that's what it might have looked like to someone else.

"Maybe you should come back another day?" the teacher said as Cora carefully scraped the blob onto a piece of cardboard.

"Oh no, this one's actually ready," Cora said.

"Oh," the teacher said. "You want to fire...that?" She placed the cardboard with the lump of clay on the drying rack prior to its firing. "If you don't mind me asking, what is it?"

"It's a pile of...you know..." Cora said, trailing off. The teacher raised her eyebrows. As Cora looked at it again, she had an idea. "Actually, wait a second." She took a pencil out of her pocket and jammed it into the top of the blob a few times. "There, now it's definitely done."

"And what is it now?" the teacher said.

"It's still a pile of...you know...but now it can hold pencils!"

● ■ ▲

If Friday had been for walking, and Saturday for ceramics, then Sunday was for dirt. Cora woke early and headed out to her small backyard garden. She had been at it a few hours when her phone rang. She was about to let the phone go to voicemail when she saw who was calling. Wiping her hands quickly on her jeans, she picked it up.

"Ray?" Cora said. "It's much too early for you to be up."

"I know!" Ray said. "And that's the rub! Here I was, sleeping a blissful slumber when my phone dinged. It was a text message from your client, Todd."

"What did he say?" Cora said.

"Nothing at first," Ray said. "It was just an emoji."

She forgot to stop herself before she asked: "What emoji?"

"Not a good one!"

"Oh no."

"Then he followed up with a text, explaining that he wasn't sending me the emoji to *send* me the emoji, he was only sending me the emoji to *show* me the emoji he'd already sent to somebody else. The text went on and on. Paragraphs! TOO LONG; DIDN'T READ! He said he'd ruined his career, but at least you were helping him." Cora sat down on the grass, shaking her head as Ray continued. "Cora, I don't want to get between you and your client, but is there something going on that I need to know about? Or is there some way I can be helpful?"

Cora launched into the story of everything that had happened with Todd over the past week. Ray made knowing noises of concern. When she was done, she let out a big sigh. That was when Ray spoke.

"Let me ask you a question, Cora. What planet do you live on?"

"Earth?" she said.

"Me, too," Ray said. "Just checking. Since I don't know much about what it's like to live on the other ones."

Cora knew enough about Ray's bizarre conversational arcs to let him run with this one. In true Ray fashion, it just might hit up against something good.

"And what do you know about life here on Earth?" Ray said.

Cora took a stab. "That it's beautiful?"

"Ha!" Ray said. "Okay, what else?"

"That it's hard?"

Ray chuckled. "Did I ever tell you about the orchestra?"

"I don't think so," Cora said.

"Well, there's this guy, and at the end of his life, he's at the pearly gates. And God's there, with his big white beard, and God says: 'So, how was it? Did you enjoy the orchestra of your life?' And the guy says, 'Well, God, I gotta say, it all would have been a lot better if it wasn't played on a crappy transistor radio!'"

Ray laughed. "Ha! That's life! A beautiful orchestra played on a radio someone probably picked up in the gutter! Or at least that's what Hermann Hesse says. I'm much older than you, and I'm old enough to tell you this, Cora. It's an imperfect mashup, this life. There's the good and the bad. The peaks and the valleys. What goes up must come down. Now, here's what I think. Your client has been living in Lala Land for too long. And I don't mean Los Angeles. He's been winning his whole life. And now he's not, and he has absolutely no idea how to deal with it." Cora nodded. She had determined as much. Ray continued. "And neither do you."

This time, she was surprised. "What?"

"How long have you been an executive coach, Cora?"

She thought back. It wasn't yet ten years, but it was more than five. She said as much.

"Good," Ray said. "Good, good. And how many clients do you think you've helped in that time?"

Cora tried. "More than thirty, fewer than fifty?"

"Good," Ray said. "Good, good. And in those years, everything's been going real nice, right? And now all of a sudden you've got this guy, Todd, who is supposed to be this tech big shot, but he's really just going around blowing up his board meetings and sending poop emojis to everyone he knows. Have you even talked to him about his allergy?"

Cora was confused now. "His allergy?"

"His allergy to change!" Ray said. "And come to think of it, he might be allergic to coaching as well."

"Right," Cora said, finally understanding. She sat silently for a while.

Ray continued. "So, do you think you're going to be able to help him?"

"I don't know," Cora said.

It hit her then, what was bothering her. The crux of it all. With every other client she'd had, she'd known she could help them. With Todd, she wasn't so sure.

CHAPTER 20

"So, are you going to tell me to apologize to everybody now?" Todd said.

He was out of bed now, hard pants on. Sitting at the desk in his home office, he stared at his email inbox as he talked to Cora.

"Do you want to apologize to people?" Cora said.

"Of course not," Todd said. "I don't *want* to apologize to anyone. But I'm old enough to know that sometimes I have to do things I don't want to do."

"And what makes you do those things?" Cora asked.

"My mortgage?" Todd said.

"True," Cora said. "Jobs are usually effective in giving us roofs over our heads. That said, most people think they have less agency in life than they really do. From everything you've said today, it sounds like you think your hands are tied."

"They are," he said. "To idiots!" Todd began to mutter under his breath.

"Todd, am I an idiot?" Cora said.

"What?" Todd said.

"Listen," Cora said. "You keep *saying* you want a coach to help you change, but you don't act that way. It seems like you're forcing yourself to do something you don't believe in. I've been patient until now, but I'm not sure you *are* coachable. Behavioral change is hard. To change a behavior, there are four stages of coaching. Being open to change, being open to feedback, being open to action, and being open to accountability. You've been stuck on that first stage for a while now, and I'm not sure you can make it out."

On the other end of the line, Cora heard frantic typing. "Todd, what are you doing right now?"

"Sorry, uh...multitasking. Another email just came in from that board member I hate. Warren. He's the worst. Sometimes I wish I could just—"

Cora interrupted. "Please close your laptop. You can tend to those after we get off the call." Todd did as Cora suggested, and she continued. "I think now is a good time for you to step back and think about the choices you have right now."

When Todd started to protest again, Cora asked him pointedly, "Do you want to be the CEO of LUNAQ?"

"What kind of a question is that?" Todd said.

"One you need to answer," Cora said. "If you want to continue as CEO, you're going to have to be open to change. Your board will make very sure of that. And I'm not sticking around unless you commit to truly being open to coaching. I think the best thing you can do today is to use some of the tools we've talked about to figure out the answer to some of these questions. For you, and for everybody else."

CHAPTER 21

After Todd got off the phone, he tried to do what Cora had told him to do. He really did. He knew he had to spend time thinking about what he wanted, and he agreed that writing about it would help him figure it out. He wasn't someone who regularly journaled, but he liked the articles Cora had sent him about how free writing was an excellent tool to help leaders untangle their biggest questions. He'd even bought a nice journal to write in.

Cora had said it helped psychologically to have one specific place to write down his questions. But his email inbox pulled at him like a magnet. Just knowing there were dozens of angry people yelling at him from inside his computer meant he couldn't think about anything else. Especially because they were wrong. The whole lot of them. He started typing.

He had agreed to check in with Cora the next day, but when he woke up and saw all the angry responses to all the emails that he'd written the day before, he didn't think he could face her. He picked up another detective novel and was about to turn off his phone when something stopped him. What was it Cora had said again? That there were key stages to making lasting change? How many was it? Five? Twenty-seven? If he was being honest, he hadn't really been listening. But he could remember the first one: being open to change. He heard his kids in the backyard, throwing a ball around. Had he even spoken to them since he'd been holed up in bed?

He threw the novel on the floor. *I can't keep doing this,* he thought. His family needed him to be better than this. *And as for LUNAQ, they might all be idiots,* he thought, *but I'm the one who is about to burn the company down to the ground.*

He texted Cora, "Can you talk? Now?"

Once on the line, he told her about his moment of clarity. It was for real this time, he said. When it came to coaching, he was finally ready to suspend belief and trust the process. For his family and his business. And she didn't have to take his word for it. He would prove it to her. After they talked more about his realization, and Cora agreed to proceed with their coaching engagement, he confessed to his latest barrage of angry emails.

"Do you think your strategy was effective?" Cora said.

"Of course not!" he said.

"And why is that?" Cora said.

"First off, because I went in wanting to fight, not to apologize. And second, because now I've just generated more noise. Things are even worse than they were yesterday. Now I have more emails to respond to and more angry people."

"So, what are you going to do instead?" Cora said.

"I'm going to write in the journal. Then I'm going on a hike to think," he said. "I'm going to figure it all out, just like you said. And then after I do, I'm going to face all those emails."

"Okay," Cora said. "And what will you do if you don't figure it out by the end of your hike today?"

"That's not going to happen," Todd said. "Because I have to."

"Todd, is this the type of decision you want to force? Yesterday, we talked about what happens when you try to force yourself to do things you don't believe in. Is this one of those times?"

"I don't have a choice," he said. "It's been days since the board meeting. I have to give them a plan!"

"What if there was another way?"

That was when Cora coached Todd to see a different path. One where he spent some time thinking and writing before calling up every board member and personally apologizing, and one in which he then gave himself a few more days to figure out a solid path forward to present to the board.

"I like it," he said, breathing a sigh of relief.

He really did.

●■▲

For the rest of the morning, Todd started in on the first part of Cora's plan. After he filled five pages of his new journal with his awful handwriting, he put the cap on his pen. If writing was thinking, then he had done a lot. He hadn't solved everything, by any means, but the panicky feeling in his chest had dissipated. Now, for a hike. Parking his car at a nearby trailhead, he shoved his phone into his backpack. Two hours later, he felt clearer.

That was when Warren sent the tweet.

Todd was unlocking his car at the trailhead when he pulled his phone out of his pack. As Cora had suggested, he'd turned it off completely for his hike, which kept him from pulling it out for a second "just to check." He had learned by now it was never just a second. He'd been pleased to find the hours without his phone to have been some of the most enjoyable ones he'd had in ages.

At the trailhead, Todd opened his email to quickly scan for urgent threats. When his inbox looked clear, he turned to his texts. Next, he went to Twitter or whatever it was they called it now. That was when he saw it. A tweet thread from his board member that, by the looks of it, was going viral. It was entitled, "Ten Ways to Deal with a Deadbeat Founder." With the character limits on the platform now extinct, Warren had a lot of space to spout off. He said that one of his founders had recently gone crazy, yelling at the board, sending crazy emails, and then going completely MIA. "To keep the founder's anonymity, we'll call him Rod," the thread said.

The tweet was blowing up.

● ■ ▲

That night, after sending one important email, Todd took his wife on a date. As they sat down at a table in a nearby Mexican restaurant, Todd reached for her hand.

"I've come to a conclusion," Todd said.

"You have?" Mira said.

"Yep," Todd said. "And it's a good one."

"Okay then, out with it."

A pop song from a famous singer, the one now dating the big athlete, was playing over the loudspeakers. One of Todd's twins loved the singer, and he played her so much it was impossible for Todd not to know some of the songs. He started to hum along.

“Todd,” Mira said. “Tell me.”

He looked at her solemnly. “I’m the problem.”

“The problem?”

“Yep. I’m the one keeping LUNAQ back from where it needs to go. It’s time for me to cut the cord and let them fly. Far away from me.”

CHAPTER 22

The next morning, Todd woke refreshed.

In a few hours, he had an emergency meeting with the board. He had convened it the night before. Since he didn't have time for a long hike, he went on a walk in his neighborhood to think about the upcoming conversation. Although he'd acted like a nutjob over the past week, it was still going to be a big surprise when he said he was stepping down. To be honest, the board members weren't going to know what hit them.

Todd was the founder and CEO, and he'd been one of the best in the game for a decade. People like Todd didn't just walk away from what they'd built. And yet that was exactly what he was going to do. Plus, he was going to do it on his terms. In situations like these, the board always asked for some sort of transition, something to assuage the employees and the investors. But he wasn't going to agree to that. He was done. And they'd just have to accept it. Hopefully, they'd do a better job of handling the announcement than Mira had the night before.

●■▲

The waiter at Antonio's was smashing two avocados into a bowl next to the table when Mira tried again to get Todd to say something, anything, that would shed more light on his sudden decision.

"Onions?" The waiter said.

"For sure!" Todd said.

"Salt and pepper?"

"I'd love nothing more!"

"Cilantro?"

"Absolutely!" Todd said. "And lime! Lots of it!" Todd smiled wider at the waiter. "What else you got?"

Todd's wife stared at him as he engaged the waiter in a discussion about how to best optimize his guacamole. Mira liked avocados as much as the next person, but she'd never seen anyone so animated. Tilting her head and scrunching up her eyes, it was obvious what she was thinking: *What the heck?* Since Todd had made his big LUNAQ declaration only ten minutes before, she'd tried to get him to tell her more about the rationale behind abruptly leaving the company he'd built. But he'd had very little to say, and he hadn't been ashamed about it. In answer to her measured questions, he'd seemed both dismissive and resigned. She'd just finished explaining that it concerned her that he had never, ever, in all their conversations, mentioned any interest in leaving LUNAQ. Didn't he think this required some more thinking? Wasn't he being rash?

Todd had looked at her blankly, sipping his margarita. That was when the waiter had arrived, and the guacamole operation had begun in earnest. She'd never seen anyone look so relieved.

"Todd, you seem so blasé about all this. You're acting like you care more about the guacamole than the fact that you're leaving the company you built and spearheaded for an entire decade. I know you've really gotten yourself into a mess, but is this the only way? And are you sure this is what you really want?"

Todd shrugged his shoulders. "I've made my bed, Mira. Now I've got to lie in it." He loaded up his chip and took a bite.

●■▲

As Todd walked around his neighborhood the next morning, he decided that if the board started to ask him a lot of questions, he'd just do what he'd done with Mira the night before: He'd shrug his shoulders. And then, when that didn't work, he'd get mad. After a lot of his shoulder shrugging over the Mexican food, Mira had brought up the conversation again on the car ride home. He'd immediately put a stop to it. "Enough!" he'd shouted. "My career at LUNAQ is done and buried, and now everyone will have to accept it."

That morning, rounding the corner to his own block, his phone buzzed in his pocket. He picked up on the second ring. It was Ray.

"Good morning!" Ray said.

"Hi Ray," Todd said. "How are you?"

"Great, great. I'm at an airport for some flight to nowhere, and I saw a small child using a telephone. Somehow, it made me think of you! How are your little emojis?"

"Thankfully, that's all sorted now."

"Glad to hear it. How'd you figure it all out?"

"You know, Ray, I just asked myself: Do I want to be dealing with this anymore? No. And then I asked: And do I need to? No and no. And that cleared it all up pretty quickly."

"Well," Ray said. "That's a clear perspective."

"Oh yeah," Todd said. "From here on out, I'm not going to do anything I don't want to do anymore. Professionally speaking. And no more dealing with people who don't think like I do."

"Is that so?" Ray said.

"No doubt!" Todd said.

"Listen," Ray said. "About this meeting you have coming up. I wouldn't want you to jump off a cliff without thinking things through. Here's my advice: Pitch a call to Cora before you quit. You hired a coach for a reason, and she just may have something to say that will help."

Todd was dubious, but this was Ray de Luca. He'd give him the benefit of the doubt. "If you say so," he said.

● ■ ▲

Cora picked up on the second ring.

"Hi, Todd. How's it going?"

"Good, good."

"Glad to hear it. How can I help?"

"Ray says I should talk to you."

"He does?"

"Yeah, yeah. But it'll just take a minute."

Cora listened while Todd explained his news. When he let out a big sigh indicating he was done, she stepped in. "That is big news, Todd. And I certainly don't need to ask if you're sure you've thought this through."

"Good," he said. "Because I have."

"I imagine. After all, there's no going back once you tell your board members what you've decided," Cora said.

"Good."

"Especially when you tell them in the way you've decided to go about it. As soon as you say everything you want to say to everyone—especially to Warren—it would be hard to work with these investors ever again," Cora said.

"I don't want to work with them again!" Todd said.

"I get it," Cora said. "I do. After all, you probably want to leave tech altogether, right? That would be perfect since it is a smaller valley than people realize, and all these investors talk."

"Well, I'm not sure I'd leave tech altogether," Todd said.

"Oh?" Cora said. "Because your plan, at least the way you've described it, sounds a lot like burning bridges. And I wouldn't want to tell you not to burn bridges—sometimes a bridge is exactly what you need to burn. In fact, it sounds like some of your investors are so awful that they deserve—"

Todd interjected, "Well, I didn't say I wanted to burn bridges. I mean, once I leave LUNAQ, maybe I will want to start another company. And some of my investors are great investors—and even greater people."

"Oh?" Cora said.

"Yeah, I mean just because we don't see eye to eye doesn't mean they are bad at what they do or that their opinions don't make sense," Todd said.

"I see," Cora said.

"It's just that we have different visions about the future of the company," Todd said.

"Got it," Cora said.

"Although not with all of them. Some of them I pretty much agree with," Todd said.

"You do?" Cora said.

"Definitely. A couple of them have interesting ideas about how I could turn LUNAQ around. I mean," Todd said, "if I wanted to, which I don't."

"Right," Cora said.

"I mean, there's this one path that Phil suggested that makes a lot of sense. I hope whoever they find next listens. The idea is genius."

"Interesting," Cora said.

"Oh yeah, it could totally fix things," Todd said. "And it wouldn't even be that hard, honestly. Although it would be difficult to find the right person to do it. It's a needle in the haystack type of thing."

"Is it?" Cora said.

"Definitely. You see, the person would need to come from a background of enterprise but with an eye toward consumer. And they'd need to come from software sales, but not just any software sales company, since most other software sales companies operate differently than we do. And they'll need to understand all the experiments we've tried already. And the current issues with the team, which are not small. But I know exactly the kind of person we need. I should probably mention this to the board members before the big meeting today. Or I guess I could tell them after today, if I'm a little softer in my delivery."

"That's an idea," Cora said.

"Honestly, I could even help find the person. I mean, I have the vision. And it might just be easier, you know," Todd said. “Since I’ve done the job before. And it’s a fun one, the job. The new person will like it. That’s also why I’d like to help find them. To make sure they see how good of a job it is. To make sure they find someone who knows what a good ride they’re about to have.”

“How lucky that you got to have it!” Cora said.

“Totally. I’ve been *so* lucky. And, honestly, in ten years, we haven’t even had many big crises. Frictions? Yes. Business challenges? Absolutely. Call me crazy, but I like those things. But crises? Nope. I mean, it’s crazy, because most start-up founders have tons of them! But not me. And not LUNAQ. Until this one.” He paused. “It’s funny because I always thought…”

“What?” Cora said.

“Well, I was going to say I always thought I was this great start-up founder. But now I’m wondering if I was only a great start-up founder because I never had to deal with any major crises. I’ve always considered myself a founder who could handle a crisis, you know? Whose feet had been held to the fire. But now…Maybe I’ve never really been tested? Maybe I’ve just had it so easy. And not just at work, but in life.”

Cora allowed the thought to sink in. “That’s a big insight,” she said.

“Yeah, and maybe me wanting to quit is just me wanting to disappear again. Wanting to turn off my phone and hide under the covers.”

“That’s interesting,” Cora said.

“Hey, did I ever tell you they used to call me The Golden Boy?”

“The Golden Boy?”

“Yeah, you know, everything he touches turns to gold?

That's what they called me in college. I even had this big blond hair back then. Star athlete. Phi Beta Kappa. And then in graduate school, it kept going. They still say it at reunions. Here comes The Golden Boy!"

"That's a big nickname," Cora said. "Some might say there's a lot of pressure behind those words."

Todd didn't hear a thing. He was in his own world now. "I've got a reunion coming up in October, actually."

"I see," Cora said softly.

"If I tried this thing, if I tried to fix LUNAQ, and it didn't work—what would they call me then?" Todd said

This time, Cora didn't answer.

CHAPTER 23

After his call with Cora, Todd had a new kind of clarity.

He didn't feel the same as when he'd thought he was going to quit. Then, he had felt light. He had felt free. But he understood now that he'd felt that way because he was escaping. This time, there was work ahead—a lot of it. There was also uncertainty. The road was going to be hard, and Todd didn't know what he didn't know yet. But he did know that he wasn't going to run from the apology tour or from the hard work of figuring out a solid path forward for the company. Now he just had to figure out what he was going to say.

He wandered out of his home office in the direction of the kitchen. Another cup of coffee would help. His wife was at the breakfast table; she was reading a book.

"I thought you went to tennis?" he said.

She pointed out the window. "Notice the weather much?"

At some point in the past hour, it had started raining. Hard. He poured himself a fresh cup of coffee and sat down to tell Mira about his conversation with Cora. She nodded along as he shared his change in thinking. When he was done, he looked at his watch.

"Well, I better get to it." He picked up his coffee cup, and as he did so, the title of the novel she was reading jumped out at him.

"*One True Thing*?"*

"An oldie, but a goodie," Mira said. "For some reason, it felt like a good day to remember."

---

* Anna Quindlen, *One True Thing: A Novel* (Random House Trade Paperbacks, 2006).

PART 3

OPEN TO ACTION

CHAPTER 24

"I'm in deep now," Todd said as he arrived at Cora's office the following week. It was on the ground floor of her home in San Francisco, and it whispered serenity from every corner. The walls were painted a grayish shade of soothing blue, and a small fountain bubbled in the corner. A wall of beautiful black and white photographs framed the room, and a big window pointed out to her garden. Todd took a seat in a plush armchair.

Cora sat down across from him, a mug of tea in front of her. "You are?" she said, without missing a beat.

"'Build a start-up,' they said. 'Grow it to unicorn,' they said. Well, it's a load of garbage if you ask me. I want out!"

Cora drew in her breath. "You do?"

"No, this time I'm kidding. Although anyone in their right mind would want out of this mess. But I'm not in my right mind!"

Todd laughed at his own joke, while Cora breathed out a sigh of relief. "Well then, I'm glad to hear we've moved on to new challenges."

"Yeah, no more Escape Room Todd. I'm in it now. In it to win it or at least to lose my mind trying. Apologizing was not easy, but I just tried to remember what Ray told me. Sometimes you have to swallow your ego and eat ___ when you don't want to eat ___."

"Eat what?" Cora said.

Todd pointed at her new pencil holder.

"It wasn't too bad, in the end."

Todd gave Cora a recap of everything that had happened in the past week, starting with the moment he had stopped rage-texting Warren and picked up the book by Peter Drucker that Ray had recommended the month before. *The Practice of Management* had helped Todd to see he was here to make a positive difference, not to prove how right he was. It had also reminded him that the people who have the power to make the decision will make the decision. In Todd's case, that was his board. After all, after many rounds of funding, Todd didn't own anywhere near the majority of LUNAQ anymore.

As Drucker explained, if Todd wanted to influence the decision-makers, then he had to treat them like customers. That meant *Todd* was the salesperson. It was a radical new way to think about his role as CEO, and it had taken a while for Todd to get his mind around the concept.

Ultimately, it had been the unlock he needed.

First, Todd had canceled that emergency meeting with the board where he planned to quit. Instead, he had called up every board member and apologized, taking ownership for all of his poor behavior: the board presentation nightmare, the outburst, the ghosting. Then he had clearly stated that he needed seventy-two more hours to think before coming back to them with a solid plan for them to consider. He knew what he was asking was unusual, but he'd told them that he believed it to be the best path forward.

The board members had each agreed, even Warren, with whom he had taken particular care. (And yes, Warren had now deleted his tweets.) Most had been on enough boards to know that some of the best companies out there had been through an all-out crisis at one time or another. They also knew that, weighing the past ten years of Todd's performance up against what they had seen recently, giving Todd a bit more time was the best of the bad options available. After three days, he'd then presented a plan. It hadn't been perfect, but it was a start.

"But I've got to say," he continued. "This is tough. Way harder than I imagined. It makes me look back on all the easy years with awe. Why didn't I appreciate what I had? But I know, no regrets."

"That's not exactly true," Cora said.

"What's not?"

"The idea that we shouldn't have regrets in life. Sometimes regrets can be useful."

"They can?"

"Sure. With some decisions, you can look back and identify where you wish you'd made a different choice. That can help you make a better one next time. The key is not to get stuck in the backward glance. You'll turn to stone. Or was it salt? Didn't somebody's wife do something in the Bible? I never did go to Sunday school..." Cora trailed off. "Point being: If you ruminate about your regrets, you'll never move forward. As Ray says, without the choices you've made, you wouldn't be you. The key to banishing regret is to make peace with your past and then be here now. So, today, let's bring it back to the now. If you had a magic wand, what is one thing you would do to help turn around the crisis at LUNAQ?"

"Well, there is one thing," Todd said.

"Yes?" Cora said.

"I'd make everybody think like me," Todd sighed. "You know what I mean?"

"I know what *you* mean," Cora said. "But think about it, Todd. Would you really want everybody to think like you?"

"Absolutely!" he said. "I really would. Then they'd know exactly what to do."

"Because you do?" she said.

Now he equivocated. "Well..."

"Todd, have you ever actually been in an escape room?"

He stared at Cora. What on earth was she on about now? "The places my kids used to go to for birthday parties? The weird little rooms with clues and stuff?"

"Yes," Cora said. "Those. Do you have any specific memories of being inside an escape room?"

"I do," Todd said.

"Great," Cora said. "That will make this even easier. We're going to do an exercise. First, you'll need to lean back in your chair and shut your eyes."

"I should probably tell you now that I don't meditate," Todd said.

"That's fine," Cora said. "Because I do."

Reluctantly, Todd closed his eyes. Cora turned on some soothing music and began to guide him on a meditation. After a few minutes of relaxation, he found himself inside an escape room. But it wasn't like any escape room he'd ever seen before. In fact, as his mind relaxed, he realized it was more like a beautiful island, with cool white sand for a floor and sparkling blue water for walls. He was on the island with a bunch of other people. Some of them he knew, some he didn't. Everyone wanted to get off the island and go home, but they couldn't figure out how. He could hear Cora's voice and the music. *Someone on the island has an idea now,* she said. *Follow that idea.* In his mind, he did. Then, he did it again. It took five tries before the group of people—his wife, his COO, his kindergarten teacher, his dead grandmother, a kid he'd never seen before—floated up and away from the island. The birds had loaned them their wings. Slowly, Cora closed the meditation.

"Weird," he said when he opened his eyes and sat up in his chair.

Cora smiled. "What was that like?"

"Weird. Did I already say that?" Todd told Cora about what he had experienced over the past twenty minutes.

"Let me ask you a question," Cora said. "How many of the ideas for escape were your ideas?"

He thought back. "Two," he said.

"Of how many, total?" she asked.

"Five," Todd said.

"Interesting," she said. "Do you know how many times I've done that exercise with clients?"

"No."

"Me neither," she said. "But I can tell you this. Not even one time has a client come up with most of the ideas."

"Huh," he said. "But aren't you going to ask me if it was my idea that got us off?"

"Nope," Cora said. "Because that doesn't matter."

"Right," he said, nodding his head. "Because bad ideas can lead to great ideas."

"Exactly. And that's the point. After reviewing the feedback from your stakeholders, I believe one of the clear things we need to work together on is the way you handle people who think differently from you. There are eight billion brains on this Earth, and no one thinks the same. That means that the people you work with, and the people who work for you, are bound to think differently from you. And that's a good thing. After all, if I were stuck in an escape room and wanted to get out, I sure as hell would want people who had different ideas than the ones I've already thought of. I think you would, too, but you may not know it yet.

"But back to your stakeholders. As we've talked about, I only get paid if you see positive change. And there are two ways to evaluate if that's taken place. First and foremost is deciding the key behaviors that will produce the most positive change for you. Second is determining the stakeholders who will decide if this change has happened. We've done the second part, but now we need to agree on the first."

Todd was stuck on something she'd said before. "So, is that what my stakeholders said about me? That I don't work well with others?"

"I wouldn't put it exactly like that," Cora said. "But your stakeholders have identified certain behaviors you engage in when you are working with people who don't think the way you do. Rigidity, stubbornness, not listening, defensiveness, and stonewalling are just some of the adjectives they used. There's a pattern." Cora looked down at her notes. "As one stakeholder said, 'At LUNAQ, when Todd is right, he is right, and when

Todd is wrong, nothing happens.'"

"I know who that was," Todd said. "The treasurer talks exactly like that. But he's a huge exaggerator, and he always sees the glass half empty. I knew I shouldn't have included him as a stakeholder. In fact, I only added him because I thought it might be nice to have something of a counter-opinion."

"They're my words," Cora said. "I always paraphrase the feedback I deliver so that my clients don't become obsessed with hunting down their detractors. In this case, I've actually combined the comments of several people."

"Oh," he said. "Well, I'm sure everyone else thought I was doing a good job. Especially given the difficult situation. After all, anyone would struggle in my shoes. And it's not as if *they* know what to do."

Cora looked at Todd this time, a small smile on her lips.

"Oh no," he said. "I'm doing it, aren't I? Exhibiting exactly the behaviors we're going to be working on? Rigidity, stubbornness—"

Cora finished the list, "Not listening, defensiveness, stonewalling..."

"I guess I have a lot more work to do than I realized."

"We all do," Cora said, "which is why it's so great that you're doing it. And I think there is something I can tell you to make you feel better. Have you ever heard of proprioception?"

"I think I learned about it in physical therapy when I broke my foot," Todd said. "It's about our sense of our body in space. Like, I'm standing in the middle of the kitchen floor, and I also have one foot on a step kind of thing?"

"Exactly, it's about sensing your body in your environment. When it's off, it's a huge problem for our physical body. But Ray uses the concept of proprioception to talk about our behaviors as well. He once read an article in *The New Yorker* where the film director Harold Ramis explained why Chevy Chase's career wasn't what it used to be. I'm paraphrasing, but the director said Chevy Chase's proprioception was off. Chevy didn't know what he was projecting to the world anymore. Combined with his superiority complex, it was a recipe for disaster."*

"It's not uncommon for successful people. Every day, the world gives them external feedback that they are doing things right: money in the bank, their face on magazine covers, people in their employ. As they rise higher, they lose touch. And they have fewer people around them who can get through to them. At its worst, a leader might wonder, 'Why change if I'm so successful?' Proprioception teaches us that people don't always know what they project to the world or how they are being perceived. Think of the old folktale, *The Emperor's New Clothes*."

"Right, right. The emperor was naked, and no one would tell him. It's like the big pop star, surrounded by sycophants, who employs all his friends and family and sees the entire world through a sheen of fame."

"Exactly," Cora said.

"The problem with people like that is they have too many Yes Men," Todd said. "None of them are willing to be honest."

"It's interesting to hear you say that," Cora said. "Because that was another concern that came up from your stakeholders."

"With me?" Todd said. "People think I have Yes Men?"

---

* Proprioception is a concept discussed by Marshall Goldsmith and Mark Reiter in *What Got You Here Won't Get You There: How Successful People Become Even More Successful* (Hachette Books, 2007).

"They do," Cora said. "It's not uncommon for CEOs at big companies. After all, you do employ the very leaders you work with, like your C-suite."

"Right, but I don't make them say what I want them to say!"

"The thing with Yes Men is sometimes they *are* being honest. It's the leader who doesn't want to listen."

"*Not listening*," Todd said, recognizing another of his problematic behaviors. "Oh no. I'm going to need to hike all the way to Hawaii to digest everything from today's session."

"It's a process. Behavioral change doesn't happen overnight. And before we start to take action, we must acknowledge and be open to what needs to change in the first place. The next stage is being open to feedback. As a coach, I use feedback from stakeholders to tell a leader, 'Hey, famous CEO, this is where you really are in the world. Now let's start to change it!' That's what I'm doing now. This is your life, Todd Turner. And we're about to change it."

CHAPTER 25

Cora was just leaving her ceramics studio when her phone rang. It was Ray.

"Check-in time!" he said.

She laughed. "Just what this coach needs." As she walked down the streets of San Francisco, she told Ray about how things had been going with Todd.

"Sounds like there's been movement," Ray said. "Movement is good."

"I guess," she said. "But not exactly up and to the right. I'm not sure how this engagement is going to end. I gave Todd his initial stakeholder feedback and my suggestions for the key behaviors we should work on, but now I think he might never talk to me again. He said he needed to go on a hike to Hawaii to digest everything."

"I hope he takes a GoPro!" Ray said.

Cora continued. "He was surprised, to say the least. And overwhelmed. And it certainly didn't seem like he wanted to process it with me."

"The feedback stage is never easy," Ray said. "Successful

people want people to like them, and it's hard to hear that they may not."

"Exactly," Cora said.

"That applies to you as well, you know."

"Huh?"

"Cora, there's never been a world-class coach who got that way by being liked by her clients. You're here to help Todd change, not to get him to invite you to his birthday parties."

"Fair enough," she said. "But I do need him to show up for another session."

"If he wants to change, he will," Ray said. "And if he doesn't, there's nothing you could have done. As I always say—"

"I know, I know. Breathe."

"Exactly. Just breathe your worries away. Life is good."

"But when will I know?" she asked.

"Ha!" Ray said. "Call me next week."

CHAPTER 26

Todd did go on a hike to think about everything. And when he was done, he was sick of himself. As chance would have it, it sounded like everyone else in his life was, too.

"Second time in a week!" one of Todd's twins said when he showed up for family dinner that night.

Mira looked sternly at their son. "Dad's trying to make some changes. Let's not make him feel bad about it."

"Sorry, you're right. So, Dad, how's the new gig?"

"New gig?" Todd said. "What are you talking about?"

"Mom said you're doing something at work you've never done before." His son held up his hands in defense. "That's all I know."

Todd looked at Mira. "She did, did she?"

"You are!" she said. "Before you were doing one thing. And now you are doing another. You don't have to change your job title to do something new."

"Fair enough," Todd said.

"So," the other son said. "How's it going?"

"Well, that's...a question," Todd said. Mira and the boys

watched as Todd twirled a long strand of spaghetti onto his fork and then untwirled it all over again. He was starting to do it again when Mira cut in.

"Does the question have an answer?"

"Not yet," Todd said. "Or at least maybe it does have one, but it's one that someone else knows—someone I haven't been listening to. Or maybe I've been dismissive. Or maybe defensive? Stonewalling?"

"Dad, what are you talking about?"

Todd put his fork down. "Let me ask you a question. Do you think I have trouble listening to people who have different opinions from me? Or do you think I ever get stubborn and only want to push my own agenda?"

"No, Dad, *never*," one son said, shaking his head. He put a hand on his heart. "Scout's honor." Todd looked relieved. Then, all three of them burst out laughing.

"What?" Todd said.

"Wait, you were serious?" the son said.

"Serious about what?"

"Uh oh," the other son said. "Who's going to tell him?"

"Let's not be mean," Mira said. She tried to keep a straight face as she placed her hand on Todd's. "Look, honey, listening to people with different opinions has never been your strong suit." She struggled for the right words. "It's just that you have such...conviction..." she trailed off.

"What Mom's trying to say—" a twin picked it up again.

"What Ryan's trying to say—" Mira said.

The other twin finally cut to the chase. "Dad, you're a mansplainer."

"A mansplainer?" Todd sat back in his chair, shock registered on his face.

"You can't be that surprised," Mira said. "You've always had a certain...authority about...things—"

"*All* things," his son Trevor clarified.

Todd jumped in. "I only have authority on a topic when I know something about it. It's not my fault I happen to be widely read and have a lot of interests or that I've been so successful—"

"False," Trevor said. "I mean, you do read, and you are successful, but you do it all the time, even when you don't know more than we do. Remember when you talked my ear off for forty-five minutes about TikTok, and you didn't think to ask if I was even on TikTok? Or, just last week, when you tried to tell me all about AI when you know nothing about it?"

"But that's not even the point," Ryan said. "So, what if you do know more about pickleball than I do? Or if your opinion is stronger? I can still have my own thoughts. It's like you shut down debate. Your way or the highway."

Ryan tried again. "At least it's usually not about stuff that's that important. It's like how to load the dishwasher or the best way to parallel park on a hill or, yeah, pickleball. I can't imagine what it would be like if it was about stuff that matters. Like, say, in a job—"

"Thank God we don't have to work for you."

Todd's face fell.

"Oops," both sons said at the same time.

Mira cut in. "I think that's enough beating up on Dad for one dinner. Why don't you guys clear your plates and go upstairs to finish your homework?"

"No, no, Mira. It's fine, really." Todd put on a brave face. "I'm the one who asked. Plus, I need the feedback." He tried to give them all one of his big smiles. "That's the whole point, in fact. As I take action to make changes, I need accountability."

After the boys went upstairs, Mira pushed her plate back and thought about the conversation they'd just had. "Let me guess. Your executive coach?"

Todd tapped his nose. "You've got it."

"I'm proud of you for what you're doing, you know. It's never easy to face up to feedback. Especially when, by definition, it's going to be about a behavior you are trying to change. But it's going to help. You *and* LUNAQ. I'm sure of it."

"That makes one of us," Todd said, swirling some more spaghetti onto his fork.

CHAPTER 27

The next morning, Todd took time off to do the thing he deemed the most important. That was something else he'd been learning from Cora: the difference between urgent and important. Although his job as a CEO obviously required his immediate attendance to company matters, it didn't mean that his entire day had to be stuck in a cycle of trigger and response. Instead, he could take time to shut off his phone and think. And it was working better than he'd expected. Although he hadn't yet found the solution to fixing LUNAQ, he knew his quiet time was putting him on the path to figuring it out—or at least in a better space to listen to one of his team members when they figured it out, he reminded himself.

Today, that important thing was licking his wounds. He'd learned the concept in one of Ray's books. Ever since Todd was a kid, he'd thought that immediately bouncing back from a setback was the way to succeed. Ray had a different tactic. He said you had to feel your feelings, that if you stuffed them down, it didn't do anyone any good. Rejected? Betrayed? Let down? Take some time to feel the emotions. Then, and only then, move forward.

Todd had asked Barbara to clear his morning calendar, and he went on a hike where he felt into all of them: the embarrassment, the rejection, the sense that his stakeholders just didn't like him. After he felt through everything, he then did something to lift his spirits. Something fun and different, something he'd been meaning to do for ages. Todd booked a tennis class.

Years ago, Todd had been good at tennis. He'd even played in college. But afterward, when there was the chance to try to go pro, he'd chosen to give it up. He didn't think he'd make it and didn't want to look like a fool for trying. At some point early in his marriage with Mira, they played a little bit together, but they'd given it up after they'd had kids. It was hard to remember why exactly. She'd picked it up again about five years ago, but he'd avoided it. Maybe it was all the distance that had made it harder to go back. Too many memories, too many disappointments and regrets, too many thoughts of what might have been.

Today, volleying with the tennis pro at their club, he tried not to think about the past. Instead, he stayed in the moment. It was fun when you did that. And the speed of the sport facilitated it. Honestly, Todd was so absorbed it was hard to think about anything at all. When he and the pro were done, they started chatting.

"So, you play a lot with my wife, Mira?" Todd said, grabbing some water.

"Mira's great. She's getting good. It's funny because when she started, I didn't think she'd be able to go very far, but she has surprised me. She just keeps at it, and she keeps getting better. Although that's not her goal, of course."

"What's her goal?"

"Fun," he said.

"And yours?"

The pro shrugged his shoulders. "This is my job. *And* I love it."

"What were you doing before this?"

"The same thing, but in Buenos Aires, where I grew up. I went pro down there, but things got complicated in the country, so I left. It hasn't been easy immigrating, but it's worked out."

"Do you miss Argentina?"

"Of course, but I'm grateful for everything it taught me."

"Like what?" Todd said.

"Well, because I'm Argentine, I'm an expert at crisis. We've gone through so much as a country that we generally know how to bounce back. Sometimes, here in the US, I look around and think, wow, these people have no idea how easy they have it. And they get really worked up about small stuff."

Todd figured it was as good a time as any to ask. "So, give me a pro tip. How do you do it? Bounce back? I've been hit with the biggest blow of my life, and I'm not exactly…bouncing."

The tennis pro patted his chest. "Resilience is a muscle, and it grows over time. Think of yourself like a tennis ball. If you're a new one, you'll bounce high when you get hit, out of control sometimes. That's because the first few times you're hit, the first few times you go through a big crisis, you're really activated. You don't know what to do, you don't know how to handle it, you're all over the place. Over time, like with used tennis balls, it takes a bigger hit to knock you, and in some ways, you respond better. You don't bounce as high; you have more control over your movements."

Todd thought about that. Admittedly, he'd never considered it a goal in life to be a used tennis ball. "I shouldn't be saying this, because the last thing I have time for is anything that does not involve sitting at my computer talking to people on videoconference calls, but...same time next week?"

They shook on it.

CHAPTER 28

The next few months saw a lot of changes in Todd's life. To the naked eye, they might not have been so obvious. He didn't sell his house, or quit his job, or get a new wife, but there was change afoot. Dinner with his family was a regular thing now. Not every night, but most nights. Date night at Antonio's had never been more frequent. Tennis was back, and hiking was here to stay. Free writing was also a tool he found himself using both at home and at work. Cora called it "journaling," even though Todd cringed at the image, the term bringing to mind a preteen girl, a pink pen in hand.

On the work front, he was also making headway. He wasn't fighting anymore, and he was putting time and energy into relationships he had fractured. He'd even gone to lunch with Warren, the board member he hated, and they'd discovered a mutual hatred for pickleball, which they both agreed was tennis for people who shouldn't ever be allowed to play tennis. There was nothing like a common enemy to bring people together.

A lot of the changes were thanks to Cora. She called this the action stage. By now, he'd memorized the framework for becoming coachable and making behavioral change: first, you become open to change, then to feedback, then to action, and finally to accountability. Slowly, her weird ways had started to seep into Todd's behavior, and Todd's stakeholders were noticing. Todd's wife had texted Cora, and the CRO, Heidi, had even asked for a meeting to discuss some of the positive changes she'd seen Todd make.

Listening better had been one of the very first behaviors he and Cora had tackled.

"It's the gateway," Cora explained during a Zoom session.

"But how do I do it?" Todd said.

He felt like a kindergartner, but he knew by now that he wasn't going to get anything out of executive coaching if he wasn't honest. Plus, as Cora reminded him often, there were no stupid questions. And when there were, she answered them anyway.

"It's hard," she said. "Really hard. But I'm going to show you."

He leaned in. "Okay," he said. "I'm ready."

And then, Cora didn't say anything. As their eyes stared at each other through the screen, the silence became uncomfortable.

"Are you going to tell me now?" he said.

"I just did," she said, sitting back with a pleased look on her face.

He'd fallen for it hook, line, and sinker.

She continued. "The best way to become a better listener is to—wait for it—*stop talking*." She shrugged her shoulders. "All you have to do, Todd, is shut up." A rare smile spread across her face. "I know, I'm a genius. You can thank me later."

It wouldn't be too long before he would.

CHAPTER 29

"Do you like my new plaque?" he said one day when Cora showed up to his office for an in-person session.

"Wow," Cora said. "I'm speechless."

She was. Before her, a grinning Todd was holding up what looked to be one of those heavy, wooden-backed diplomas they pass out when you spend half a million dollars to get a fancy degree. She knew them well. She even had a few of them hanging in her bathroom. But this one was different. She narrowed her eyes to read the small gold letters.

Todd Turner

Works well with others!

An aspirational MBA in shutting up!

"It's so accurate...and cheeky."

"Oh, my kids are nothing if not cheeky."

"They made it?"

"Yep. And I've never been prouder. After I started taking action to listen better, the next stage was accountability. This helps remind me."

Todd explained that when it came to working better with

people, shutting up really did make a difference.

"There's something interesting going on. When I shut up more, I hear more good ideas. It's kind of crazy, honestly. I'm like, were they out there, just floating around, but my ears didn't catch them? Or were they not voiced? It's like the thing about the tree falling in the forest with no one around—"

Cora finished his thought, "If an idea comes out of someone's mouth, and there is no leader around to hear it, was it really thought of at all?" She settled into her seat across from Todd. He had ordered two different warm beverages for her, and her eyes darted excitedly from one to the other. "There are a few different things going on. The first thing is that your ears are larger now." She lowered her voice. "Elephantitis of the leader."

He looked startled. "What?"

"Not really," she said. "But it probably feels that way. You've opened the floodgates, and more things are coming in. Most people speak to fill the void. You've given them one, and they're jumping in. Plus, you're probably experiencing the effects of the Red Car Theory, or the frequency illusion. As soon as you really notice something—like a red car—you'll start seeing it everywhere. It's a type of cognitive bias related to attention. It seems to be a combination of selective attention and confirmation bias. When it happens, it's wild."

"Exactly. It's like I have a totally different filter."

Cora leaned back in her chair, a drink in each hand. "So, tell me about the Post-it notes."

Todd was cradling his wooden diploma, and she could see a series of Post-it notes tacked to the back. Each note only had a word or two on it, and some of them were crossed off. As she looked closer, she began to read them out loud.

"Not listening, defensiveness, rigidity, stubbornness, stonewalling—oh, that one's crossed off. Is that good or bad?"

"Good, definitely good," Todd said.

"It's all your problematic behaviors, and in one place!"

"Yeah, it's kind of a downer, but it does remind me of what I'm working on."

"What's on deck for this week?"

"Back to rigidity, unfortunately. There's been some backsliding..."

Cora smiled. "That's okay. In my experience, progress isn't always up and to the right."

CHAPTER 30

In their next session, Todd circled back to the topic of regrets. He was having trouble accepting the mistakes of his past and was having even more trouble learning from them without ruminating on them. He kept wanting to look back.

"Nobody said it was going to be easy," Cora said.

"I just can't stop sometimes," Todd said. "Thinking about everything I did wrong."

"Which particular regret keeps grabbing you?"

"The one about running away when things get hard. It's easy to do, but it's hard to come back from. At LUNAQ, I'm still working to win back the trust of some of the board members who lost confidence in me when I went MIA."

"It sounds like you have a good attitude about it. Trust is easy to break and hard to rebuild, but both of those things happen all the time. How high on your list of concerns is rebuilding your trust with board members these days?"

"Very high," Todd said. "Especially because I need their networks more than ever to fill a glaring leadership hole in my C-suite."

"Oh boy," Cora said. "What happened?"

"What happened is I need a new COO," Todd said, sighing. "It's a long story."

"I've got time," Cora said.

And so, Todd told her.

The COO, Andrew, was an old friend of Todd's and had been at LUNAQ since the beginning. Their closeness had made it easy for them to work together for a long time. But during the past year, as things became tougher at the company, he hadn't been performing as well as Todd had hoped. At the same time, the CRO, Heidi, the one who had stepped in to save what Todd had tried to destroy during that disastrous board meeting, had proven to be a rising star.

As Heidi had gained more visibility and power in the organization, Andrew had started to resent it, which was ironic, because Heidi had been taking on the very things that Andrew was supposed to have been handling. He'd even told Todd as much, bemoaning how much fun they'd had back in the "good old days."

When everything had happened at the board meeting, and when Todd had gone MIA, Andrew had been supportive. Too supportive, perhaps. He'd agreed with almost everything Todd had done. Andrew hadn't wanted the company to change, and he hadn't wanted the board to make it change. When Todd had decided to change, and had realized the company needed to as well, Andrew had not been able to get on board.

"The changes in the past few months were too much for him," Todd said. "I knew they might be. No matter how much I tried to convince him, he couldn't see that LUNAQ needed to enter a new era. That *we* needed to change. He kept espousing this weird toxic positivity, saying everything would be fine if we could only put our heads down and go back to the way things were. But everything is not fine! It hasn't been fine for a long time! Ultimately, I had to let him go."

"It sounds like it was a tough decision, but it also sounds like you handled it remarkably well," Cora said.

"I felt proud of myself. No small credit to Ray, of course."

"Did you talk to Ray about it?"

"No, but I'm reading another of his books. In it, there was something that stuck with me. He says people can only change if they have the internal motivation to do so. You and I have also talked about that idea. I started to wonder if an organization is similar. A company that wants to change needs a C-suite internally committed to doing so. After all, how can LUNAQ turn itself around if its number two executive is dragging his feet?"

"It can't," Cora said.

"Exactly. So, now I'm looking for someone new. It's going to be tough. It would be so much easier if I had someone internally with enough experience."

"And you don't?"

"Oh no, I need someone much more senior. The COO role is a big step up from the rest of the C-suite positions. No one in my C-suite right now has done the job before."

"Have you?"

"What do you mean? Have I been a COO?"

"No, I mean, have you done your job before?"

"Sure," he said. "I've been a CEO for ten years."

"And before that?"

"Well, no," he said. "I learned it all on the job."

"Interesting," Cora said. "And what about this iteration of

your CEO role? The turnaround CEO? Have you ever done the job you're doing right now?"

Todd was reminded of what Mira had said to him at dinner, about having a new job. "You're not the first person who has said I'm in a new role," he said. "But I'm still not sure what you're getting at. Do you want me to hire someone who hasn't been a COO before?"

"I don't *want* you to do anything," Cora said. "But I am asking you if you are being too restrictive about the candidates you'd consider for the position. You said yourself that you wish you could promote someone internally. Maybe that's a desire worth exploring."

"Maybe," Todd said half-heartedly. He wasn't so sure.

CHAPTER 31

"I was right, and she was wrong, and now I don't know what to do," Dale said through the pixelated Zoom window. Through his screen, Todd could see Dale scrunched up on some kind of collapsible chair. He saw a headless arm hand Dale a Dixie cup of something blue. Todd knew it was blue because he watched through the screen as it fell on Dale's face.

"Oh no!" Dale said, knocking his phone, and Todd, to the grass. "Does anyone have a towel?" Someone handed Dale a towel, and now Todd was being wiped. "Sorry about that," Dale said, now crumpled back up in his chair.

"So, you were saying…" Todd tried, but the video cut out, yet again.

It was Saturday morning, and Todd (and Dale) were working.

"—then I told her that wasn't going to happen," Dale said. His connection was bad, he'd explained, because he was at a soccer game. He continued, "She didn't like it, that's for sure, but she fixed the problem."

"That sounds positive," Todd said, trying to wrap things up.

He wasn't following whatever was left of this mess of a conversation. He held up his watch to his face, so he could be sure Dale would see the gesture. "Well, I think it's about that time—"

"Is it? But how many more problems will they have to fix? It was so much easier when Andrew was around. She always listened to our COO."

"She did?"

"Oh yeah. The finance department hates me; they always have. Finance always hates marketing. You try to explain brand marketing to someone who once actually enjoyed calculus. What seventeen-year-old liked—"

"GOAL!"

Dale's phone was in the grass again, and Todd was now watching Dale's dirty cross-trainers hop up and down. There was a scuffle, and then Dale was back.

"Congrats!" Todd said.

"Too bad it went into their own goal again. Sometimes they get going in the opposite direction," Dale shrugged his shoulders evenly. "But what can we expect? They're three!" Suddenly, he remembered the conversation he was having with his boss. "So, what should I do?"

"What should you do?" Todd said. He had forgotten why they were talking in the first place.

"Yeah, Andrew always told me how to handle finance. He always told me what to do."

Dale was a good leader. Quirky, but good. And someone probably needed to help Dale. But that someone wasn't Todd. Over the past two weeks, Todd had been drowning. It turned out that losing your COO in a time of crisis was, well, another crisis. Suddenly, Todd had double the meetings he'd had before.

And the new ones were all with senior executives who had reported to his COO. Again and again, one thing had stood out to Todd. A heck of a lot of the time, his executives did not know what to do. And worse, they wanted him to tell them what to do. About everything!

"It's like they haven't been enabled to make their own decisions," Todd told Cora when he spoke to her that week. "The COO had them on a tight leash, and now that's been cut, and they're out there flailing. They don't know how to act alone! And I'm stuck with them. I don't need to tell you that that's the last thing I have time for. What the hell was Andrew thinking? And how could I have kept him around so long if he was perpetuating this?"

"Hold on there. Behavioral patterns usually start with bad habits. And there are some common ones that may have led to this," Cora said. "For example, as the CEO, have you ever been pulled into a meeting with the design team, and you start wondering out loud if everything might look better in blue? And then two days later, everything is blue, and you start thinking red might be better?"

"It was green and yellow," Todd said. "But yes."

"Exactly. Leaders often have a bad habit of verbalizing everything they think. You thought you were just throwing out ideas, but your direct reports see them as commands. The problem gets worse the higher up a leader goes. That's why leaders should keep themselves from verbalizing every thought that comes into their head."

"And you think that happened with Andrew?"

"Maybe. And once it happens enough times, your direct reports stop wanting to do anything on their own. It's a cycle."

Cora nodded. "And then there's the elephantitis."

"Oh no. Not that again."

"I'm only bringing it up again because I'm worried it's catching. It's great how much you are listening to others these days, but I also want you to be aware of over-correcting. It's one of the most common things we do as humans when we want to fix something. Before, you weren't listening enough. Now, you're listening too much. That whole story? Your head on the grass, the Gatorade on your face, the jumping up and down. Would the old Todd have stayed on that call?"

"Absolutely not."

"And we both know why the new Todd did. You're over-correcting. And you're probably trying to win back some of your detractors."

"Guilty as charged."

"Let me ask you another question. Do you trust your leaders?"

"Yes," Todd said. "I do."

"Then operate at the speed of trust," Cora said.

"Is that something else Ray says?" Todd said.

"Actually, this time it's Stephen M. R. Covey," Cora said. "The son of the more famous Covey. If you trust your executives, you should trust what they will do when they are forced to make a decision alone."

"Alone?"

"Alone," Cora said.

"And how do I get them to do that?" Todd said.

"Easy," Cora said. "You tell them. Andrew's gone, folks. New rules, new business."

At the risk of feeling positive, Todd thought it just might work.

CHAPTER 32

The next time he spoke with Cora, Todd had good news.

"Remember the speed of trust thing?" he said.

"Of course."

"Well, it's working. Take Dale, the CMO. I told him to work things out with finance by himself from now on. He was worried at first because Andrew had always handled the relationship, but he did it anyway. The initial interaction wasn't the smoothest thing in the world, but they eventually figured it out. And now I'm not a kindergarten cop."

"Great," Cora said. "You hired good people. It's time to sit back and let them do their work."

"Agreed," Todd said. "Also, it got me thinking about something else."

"Yes?" Cora said.

"You asked me the other day if I trusted my C-suite. I said I did. I do. And then you said that if I trust them, I should trust what they will do. That's what made me think. Remember when you said I hadn't ever been the CEO of a turnaround before, but here I am? Maybe I have been too restrictive in terms of my search for a COO. I've been limiting it to folks who've been in that role before, but we're not having much luck. Our recruiters and our board have pounded the pavement, but no great candidates have risen to the top. And I really need to fill the position. So, that gave me an idea."

"Yes?"

"The idea is to go internal."

"Who are you thinking?"

"The CRO, Heidi."

"Interesting," Cora said. "Walk me through your thinking."

"Well, she's great. You may remember some of this, but she was the CRO of a smaller company, and I recruited her. And it's true, she's only been in the C-suite at a company of our size for a year or so, but she's doing fantastic. I always knew she was capable, but after Andrew left, it became even clearer to me that I hadn't allowed her to really blossom. And so, I wondered."

"You wondered if you could promote her."

"I did."

"What more do you need to know to make your decision?"

"That's the thing," Todd said. "Usually, I'm quick and dirty with decision-making. But this time, it's different. This time, I'm not sure yet."

"That might not be a bad thing," Cora said. "But it's important to understand why you're not ready to pull the trigger yet. Have you been crowdsourcing too many opinions?"

"Not at all. In fact, I've barely talked about it."

"Are you being deliberate in a way that is overcorrecting? You've said that your decisions are usually quick and dirty. Are you trying to go too far in the other direction?"

"I don't think so."

"Are you hiding from the decision?"

"No."

"So, what do you think it is?"

"I think I'm honestly just…not sure yet."

"Is that stressful?"

"No," Todd said. "I have the sense I *will* know, but I just don't yet."

"It sounds like you've put it on the back burner," Cora said. "And I love back-burnering."

"Is that a word?"

"It should be," Cora said. "It's like a pot on the stove. You prepared it with all the right ingredients, and now it just has to simmer. You don't even have to tend to it. Instead, you can wait to see what emerges."

"I like it," Todd said. He did. "But how will I know when it's ready?"

"Oh," Cora said. "You'll know."

CHAPTER 33

It only took a month to prove that promoting Heidi to COO was the smartest thing Todd had done at LUNAQ in ages. She took to the new role like a fish to water; she navigated management and execution while also inspiring trust and confidence in the team. She also had a unique ability to guide and delegate in equal measure. Under her leadership, Todd saw how many of the behaviors he had been working to improve were already things she innately knew how to do. There were times that he couldn't help but think she was more of a natural at leadership than he was. He loved leading, but he wasn't sure it had ever been so easy for him. She also possessed an energy and enthusiasm that he simply couldn't muster anymore. Was he too old already? Too jaded?

He had even taken the time to ask some of the other C-suite members their impressions of the promotion. He wasn't entirely sure what his aims were with his questions, but he knew he needed to ask them. Did they see what he was seeing? Universally, they saw Heidi's move to COO as a big, positive step. The feedback sounded exactly like what Cora had taught him good feedback should be: measured and thoughtful, not from the mouths of sycophants.

"She's not afraid to lay down the line," the treasurer said.

"She's tough and kind," the general counsel said.

"When she knows something, she knows it. And when she doesn't, she tells you," the CMO said.

He explained it all to Mira over dinner at Antonio's. Todd loved how much they were getting out of these date nights. Plus, more guacamole!

"She sounds fantastic," Mira said. "Does it ever make you jealous?"

"Of what?"

"Well, some leaders in your position might be jealous that someone more junior is having so much success and seems like more of a 'natural,' as you put it. Something I don't agree with, by the way."

"Thanks for that, but I'm right this time. She *is* more of a natural. And no, I'm not jealous anymore," Todd said. "I'm thrilled!"

"Interesting," she said.

"What does that mean?" he said, laughing. "That's a Cora word, and whenever she says it, there's always something more behind it."

"Well, it *is* interesting. As soon as you overcame your personal jealousy, you were able to see her true strengths and how they could be applied to the shared mission. It's good information to keep on the back burner."

"The back burner!" he said.

"What?" Mira said.

"You and Cora. Great minds."

CHAPTER 34

Later that week, Todd was singing the same song; this time, to Cora. "She's just such a natural!" he said, a delighted smile on his face.

"I'm glad that promoting Heidi to COO has been such a good decision for the company," Cora said. "But I do want to double-click on something you've said to me a few times now. This whole idea of her being a 'natural' leader. Are you familiar with Carol Dweck's mindset work?"

"The Stanford researcher, right?" Todd said. "Remind me again?"

"Dweck's research has shown that there is a growth mindset and a fixed mindset. Someone with a fixed mindset believes he has innate traits that can't change or grow. Someone with a growth mindset believes the opposite. In just one example, Dweck recommends that parents avoid using fixed qualities to praise kids. Instead of saying, 'Wow, kid, you are so smart at math!' a parent would be better off saying, 'Wow, kid, you are working so hard at math.' That way, the child doesn't see being 'good at math' as a fixed state she was either born or not born with. Instead, she learns how important it is to put in work to get better.

"As a behavioral coach, I would hope that our time together so far has shown you that people can not only learn new things, like math, but they can also change their behaviors. It takes internal motivation, and a lot of work, but people do it all the time. As we've talked about, it requires four things: openness to change, feedback, action, and accountability. When you mention Heidi, I notice some black-and-white thinking. She is good, you are less good. I don't see the situation like that."

"Fair enough," Todd said. "But it's a good thing she's so good. I'm praising her. I'm thrilled!"

"I see that, I do. But what happens when it's time for *her* to work on something to make herself into a better leader? We all need to work on things after all. Or, God forbid, what happens if she makes a mistake? And what if it's a big one?"

Sometimes, Todd thought, Cora needed to take some of her own medicine.

The woman worried far too much.

CHAPTER 35

Heidi fell off the pedestal soon enough. It was the executive off-site that did it, three months into her promotion.

It all started with the trust falls.

"I'm not doing that," she said under her breath to the CMO when the ropes course facilitator said it was time to do something that "tested the limits of their interior sense of deep-down knowing."

"Look, I did the rope bridge. I did the tree climbing. But I don't want to do that," she said, pointing to another group of executives standing below a platform where the general counsel was about to dive off.

The CMO shrugged his shoulders. He liked the trust falls. Heidi took a seat on a nearby bench under the redwoods, answering emails on her phone while the executives around her cheered and laughed. After the trust fall, there was another group activity.

"The trees are calling, Heidi!" shouted the facilitator.

"Something important has come up," she pointed to her phone. "I'll catch up with you all at lunch."

At lunch, she was seated at a picnic table with Todd and the CMO.

"Have heights always scared you?" Todd said.

"Huh?" Heidi was on her phone again. "Sorry, I just need to answer this quickly." It took her more than a minute to tap out a long response. Todd wondered if they needed a basket for her phone.

"I was asking if heights have always scared you," Todd said when Heidi finally put her phone face down on the table.

"No, I like heights. I've been skydiving a few times."

"Oh, I thought that was why you stepped out of the activities?"

"It wasn't that. I just had some emails to answer."

Todd thought about that. He also had emails.

It was the CMO who said it: "Don't we all have emails to answer?"

"Well, maybe you should be answering them," she said.

The CMO gave her a strange look. Then he laughed. "Totally!" he said. "Good one!"

She started, and then smiled, easing into a forced chuckle; she hadn't meant it as a joke.

For the rest of the day, Todd kept an eye on her participation. She held back, that was for sure. Under the trees, without a work problem to manage, she seemed reserved and adrift. It was almost as if she didn't know how to interact with her coworkers and direct reports outside the office. Had he never realized how shy she really was? One of Todd's twins was painfully shy, so he wouldn't fault Heidi for that. But he did fault her for something else. It didn't take much to see that Heidi, in her helmet, under the tall redwoods with LUNAQ's executive team happily chattering around her, looked miserable. She was the number two person at the company! This was their executive offsite! And it was abundantly clear to anyone who was paying attention that she didn't want to be there at all.

Later that week at the office, he talked with her about it.

"I am an introvert," she said. "Also, I can be shy." Todd had guessed as much. He didn't think every leader needed to be the life of the party. "At work, it's easy for me to know what to say because the context helps organize our social interactions," she continued. Todd nodded, but he didn't fill the space. Instead, he kept listening. "To be honest, though, I guess a part of me didn't want to be there in the first place. I don't really believe in all that, you know? We have so much to do, I think we just need to do it. Do we need to bond? Or do we just need to hustle and grind? You know what I mean?"

Todd did know what she meant. And at one point in time, he used to think like she did. But not anymore.

He talked with Cora about it at their next meeting.

"Sounds like a case of goal-setting-itis," Cora said.

"Is this related to the elephant ears?" Todd joked.

Cora cracked a rare smile. "Goal-setting-itis is when the goal becomes so important to someone that they can't see anything else. In Heidi's case, she's laser-focused on LUNAQ's success and thinks that she can only achieve that by grinding in the way she's always grinded. She doesn't see that building and strengthening relationships with her team outside the office is essential. Or that taking a break from work will make her productive. She can't see the forest for the trees. Have you ever heard about the Good Samaritan study on goal obsession?"

"Nope," Todd said.

"It was a famous study done at Princeton back in the 1970s. The researchers told a group of theology students that they were going to deliver a sermon on the Good Samaritan. The hitch was that the sermon was on the other side of campus, and some of the students were told they were late and needed to hurry. They thought people were waiting for them. Along the way, the researchers had hired an actor to play someone who needed help—he was suffering, coughing and such. Ninety percent of the students ignored the needs of the person to get to their talk in time. A few times, a student literally stepped over the person in pain to get to the talk in time. Their talk about being a Good Samaritan!"*

"Wow," Todd said.

"That's goal obsession," Cora said.

"So, Heidi is stepping over the very colleagues she needs to work well with to reach LUNAQ's goals?"

"Something like that," Cora said.

"Too bad I didn't hire someone who could understand the big picture."

"Maybe," Cora said. "But maybe not. Everyone has things to work on. If you had hired someone who wasn't so goal-obsessed, that person probably wouldn't know how to listen well, or how to give critical feedback, or how to positively recognize people for a job well done. There are tons of behaviors that trip up leaders, and we all exhibit some of them. Ultimately, if she's motivated to change, she can fix it."

---

* John M. Darley and C. Daniel Batson, "From Jerusalem to Jericho: A Study of Situational and Dispositional Variables in Helping Behavior," *Journal of Personality and Social Psychology* 27, no. 1 (1973): 100–108, https://doi.org/10.1037/h0034449.

"Right," Todd said. "Like with me. But how do I know if she's motivated or not?"

"You won't. But Lynn will."

"Lynn?" Todd said. Then he remembered he'd seen this movie before. Lynn must be the coach Cora had in mind. He chuckled. "So that's her name?"

CHAPTER 36

Cora and Ray were seated in Ray's backyard, kombucha in hand, the San Diego sun shining brightly as always. A few times a year, Cora flew down to spend time with Ray. She also liked to keep an eye on everybody else. Things were much as Cora had left them a few months ago. Ray's wife was in an orange phase—all orange paintings, all the time—and Raybot was the same as ever, grumpy and in need of a new operating system. The grandkids weren't there—"Thank God," Ray said—but tiny, stray socks littered the house, evidence of a recent visit.

"My former child dropped the kids off last night, entirely unsupervised. The urchins made me order pizza," Ray said. "By the time it came, they'd decided they hated pizza."

Cora laughed. "Grandfather of the year."

Ray toasted Cora. "I wouldn't have it any other way."

Cora started to tell Ray about her client work over the past few months. She enjoyed the listening ear and asked for guidance where she needed it. She kept coming back to Todd.

"That feeling at the beginning was an awful feeling," she said. Ray nodded. "But once I knew it was fear—fear I wouldn't succeed as a coach—it became easier to deal with."

"That's the beauty of acknowledging your feelings," Ray said, sitting back in his chair. "It's always worse when we don't know *why* we feel the way we feel. When we do, we can feel it. Then, after we do, we can remind ourselves that feelings aren't facts, and that bad feelings and good feelings are both part of the human condition. Life isn't all rainbows and pony rides."

"Exactly," Cora said. "It also helped me when I realized how much I was taking my people-pleasing tendencies into my client work."

"People-pleasing tendencies?"

"Oh yes," Cora said. "I'm a big people pleaser!"

Raybot was down for a nap, but Ray could hear the robot's voice screaming in his head. *No-affect, never-smile Cora? Three-point-two-scoops-matcha-oat-milk-no-sugar-low-foam-extra-large-cup Cora? Woman-of-no-preamble-who-always-says-exactly-what-she-thinks-Cora? A people pleaser? Yeah, right!*

"It's something I'm working on with Soon," Cora said. "The coach you recommended."

Ray shrugged his shoulders. He was free-range now, he reminded himself. He didn't have to get involved in *everything*. And self-reflection was a process. He sat back in his chair and raised his glass.

"To *not* people pleasing," he said.

CHAPTER 37

"You want to take me to the orthodontist? But that's a mom thing," Todd's son Trevor said when he picked him up early from school.

"I was thinking about it, and I think it should be a dad thing, too," Todd said. "Change can be a good thing."

His son took that in. "I've got to say it, Dad. You seem to be doing better at life these days. And you seem happier. I think this new job fits you."

After the orthodontist, Todd drove them to a café that his assistant's Gen Z daughter had recommended.

"You like Boba tea, right?" Todd asked.

"Who doesn't love Boba?" Trevor said.

"Exactly!" Todd said.

They got their drinks, which Todd noted cost more than the rent on his first apartment, and they sat down at a little table outside. The sun was shining. Todd took a few easy sips before he began to struggle with a ball of something gelatinous in his right cheek. His son was in a similar boat.

"Wow, it's so...chewy," Todd said.

"Yeah," his son said. "So much…texture."

Todd set his drink down and looked at his son. "The only problem with Boba," he said, "is the Boba."

"Exactly," his son said, "too much Boba."

"Should we get going?"

They dropped the rest of their drinks in the trash and started walking back to the car.

"But it was good in theory," Todd said.

"Totally," his son said.

"So," Todd said, "I read about this summer class for middle schoolers with some genius AI guy. I thought you might want to do it. I know you have other stuff going on, but maybe it's worth looking into."

"Wow. Sounds super cool. Thanks for thinking of it. But what about Ryan?"

"Don't worry, I found something else for him up in Oregon. A Shakespeare thing."

"Is this all because of some book you read about being a better father?"

"Yeah," Todd said. "Is it working? Because if it's not, I'd love to know before I spend a fortune sending you guys to these camps."

"No, no, let's definitely do the camps," Trevor said. "So, what's the book say about Mom?"

"Oh, I've got that covered. I'm taking Mom to dinner tonight. Date night."

"To Antonio's?"

Todd nodded. "Yep. Why mess with a good thing, right?"

Trevor let out a sort of strangled, wheezing noise; almost, but not quite, a cough.

"Got some Boba stuck in there?" Todd said.

"No, it's just..."

"What?"

"Well..."

"Tell me."

He blurted it out. "Mom says it's too much Mexican."

"Is there such a thing?" Todd said, with genuine confusion. And then, "What else does she say?"

His son drew in a breath. "Mom says you're a one-trick pony when it comes to date night." He paused and then continued. "Mom says you can't see the big picture. Mom says that one geographically convenient Mexican joint has blinded you to the rest of the gastronomic wealth of the San Francisco Bay Area, which is inclusive of Mexican food, but not restricted to it. Mom says she is wasting away culinarily but doesn't want to add to the list of your worries, which is long, admittedly. Mom says she has no problem divorcing you if you make her go to Antonio's every Thursday for the rest of her life."

"Wow, Mom said all that?" Todd said. "Good thing I'm well-versed in taking in negative feedback now."

● ■ ▲

As Todd was getting ready to leave the house for dinner that night, Mira still wasn't home. He called to see where she was.

"Remember, dinner's at six thirty," he said.

"Antonio's is just down the block from the gallery, so I'll just meet you there."

"No, we're headed somewhere else. Let's go together."

"Wow, I was really hoping for Mexican," Mira said with no

enthusiasm whatsoever. Todd wondered if he had ever heard anyone sound less genuine. Was this what she had always sounded like when he suggested Antonio's? And he'd just never listened to it?

Seventy-five minutes of bumper-to-bumper traffic in an Uber later, Todd was smooshing some smoked fish onto a piece of rye bread at a Scandinavian place he'd found on the fifth page of a Google search he now regretted.

"Is it supposed to be so dry?" He'd asked. "My...breakfast?"

"Todd," Mira said, giving him a warning look.

After two shots of pure vodka chased by one lone caper, things brightened, and they began to discuss some of the changes in Todd's work life over the past year.

"Seems like it's going great," Mira said. "I never thought I'd say this, but the new LUNAQ suits you better than ever. Maybe you should work there forever!"

Todd looked down at his caper. He gave it a funny look.

CHAPTER 38

It had been almost a year since the board meeting from hell, and things at LUNAQ were looking up. Nothing was perfect, not by a long shot. But with the strides Todd had made as a leader, Heidi's promotion, and the positive changes Heidi had been making with her executive coach, things were in a good place. A good enough place that Todd felt looser these days. There was a lightness in his step, and there was more margin in his mind. He could decide to take his kid to the orthodontist on a Tuesday, he could plan longer hikes, he could Google better Nordic food. He no longer felt like he was walking around the world and hugging a grenade. He was no longer hoping against hope that the grenade wouldn't explode in his hands before he told everybody to clear out.

He was even starting to think of new possibilities.

● ■ ▲

One day, he was speaking to Heidi in his office about the upcoming board meeting. It was a big one, and they aimed to deliver early results on the turnaround and all the changes to the business.

"I think we're pulling it off, and I think *you* should talk about it," Todd said.

"Me?" Heidi said.

"Yep. It's your show," Todd smiled. She looked at him doubtfully. "Trust me on this," he added.

● ■ ▲

In Todd's office a week later, Heidi pulled up the slide deck on her computer. She had asked to practice her upcoming presentation with him. It would be her first to the board as COO, and she wanted to make sure it was great.

"We're not in the clear yet," she was saying to an audience of one. "Not by a long shot. But the early signs of product market fit with the new AI solution are impressive, and they indicate a whole new consumer angle to the business that could be a huge win. This doesn't mean we'll be ignoring our enterprise clients anytime soon, but we will be learning to find a balance. I know that's not always easy. One of our biggest risks moving forward will be making sure we don't spread ourselves too thin. Which is why we've made a few decisions to mitigate the..."

As Todd watched her, he could imagine her fielding the questions the board would have. Warren would pipe up first, as always, with something that came off as brash. Heidi would take it in stride, knowing it was his style to come off as the snarky one in the room when he was really all heart. The telecom executive would then cut in, asking a hard question, but lightening it up with a self-deprecating joke. Heidi would think about what she'd said and respond with consideration. Someone in the back would be confused by something and want clarification. Heidi would explain it again, carefully, with new words. In Todd's mind, he could see her energy as she commanded the room. He could see her control, her mastery. All kinds of problems stood in front of them, but he knew she could face them.

Looking at her, he had the sense of something about to begin.

PART 4

OPEN TO ACCOUNTABILITY

CHAPTER 39

It wasn't a quick decision this time.

Nearly a year earlier, when Todd had first wanted to leave LUNAQ, it only took an hour for him to decide to quit. The board member had angered him, and he was out. *Rage quitting*, his twins had explained to him later. He wasn't proud of what he'd done, not by a long shot, but these days he couldn't help but long for that kind of clarity. Because this time around, he was stuck. He'd gone back and forth. He'd made the pros and cons lists. He'd talked to his wife and Cora, ad nauseam. Finally, he called up Ray.

"So, what should I do?" he said after he explained the situation and his thinking.

"Don't ask me," Ray said. "It's your life."

"But how am I going to decide?"

"I don't know," Ray said. "But I can ask you some questions that might help."

"Okay," Todd said. *Cora had already asked him all the questions*, he thought, but didn't say.

"First, tell me about what you're scared to lose by walking away."

"What am I *not* scared to lose?" Todd said. "The money, the status, the success."

"We've talked about your money before," Ray said. "And I know there won't be a problem putting food on the table. I'm taking that one out. Agreed?"

"Agreed," Todd said.

"So, status and success. Those are hard things to say goodbye to," Ray said.

"They are," Todd said. "Who doesn't like showing up at TED and knowing you're going to be on stage?"

"It's true. That's why some people only walk away if they have internal conviction pointing them in a new direction. You haven't told me yet. If you quit, is there something else you want to do instead?"

"Not that I know of," Todd said. "Honestly, I'm not sure what I'll do if I leave."

"I'm not going to lie to you," Ray said. "Leaving comes with risk. You might fail at coming up with something else to do. You might fail at doing the thing you eventually do come up with. All of that might suck. How willing are you to lose what you have?"

"I'm not sure," Todd said.

"You'll want to figure that out," Ray said. "But there's also one more thing to throw into your magic decision pot before you swirl things around."

"What's that?" Todd said.

"We've only talked about the risk of leaving. There is just as much risk involved in standing still."

Todd made a noise. "In my case, I don't think there's much risk in continuing with the status quo. LUNAQ is doing well.

My role is stable. Nothing's going to change anytime soon."

"Don't kid yourself," Ray said. "The only predictable thing about life is that it's unpredictable. Mark my words. There's just as much risk in *not* making a decision as there is in making one."

CHAPTER 40

The next day, Todd drove up to the Marin Headlands. He and Cora were going on a hike.

"But I'm not a hiker," she'd clarified prior to the hike. "I really *like* hiking, but I don't consider it part of my athletic identity."

"Got it," Todd had said.

"And I'm not particularly adept," she'd said.

"Got it," Todd had repeated.

"I don't walk fast." Todd had nodded. "And I don't carry a little bottle," she'd added.

"No bottle."

●■▲

When he pulled up to the trailhead, she was waiting for him.

"Can we talk now?" He said when he got out of the car. "Or has it already started?"

When Cora had proposed the hike, she'd explained that this wasn't just any hike: it was a silent hike. They were not going to talk to each other.

"We've talked enough," she'd said. "When we get there, I want you to be inside the world of the hike. And inside the world of the hike, you've already quit LUNAQ. While you're walking, I want you to feel into that world."

"Sounds weird," he'd said. "But it's worth a shot."

Two hours after first trudging up the reddish-brown trail into the tall trees, they were back at the trailhead. Cora was greedily gulping water out of the fountain, and Todd leaned back on a post.

"Yesterday, Ray asked me if I was feeling some kind of internal conviction pushing me to leave LUNAQ."

"Interesting," Cora said.

"I told him that I wasn't. As you know, I have no idea what I might do next."

"Right," Cora said.

"But the hike showed me I was wrong about the conviction. Because I am feeling that."

"You are?" Cora said.

"Yep," Todd said.

"And what is that conviction?" Cora said.

"I'll tell you tomorrow."

CHAPTER 41

The next day, Todd's schedule was virtually clear. He had asked his executive assistant to cancel all his meetings but one. The important one. The call itself would be short, but Todd knew by now that the shortest books took the longest to write. He did the things that had long become habits for him. He wrote some notes in his journal. He went on a walk without his phone. As he did, he thought about what a positive difference Cora had made in his life. Ray had as well, but it was Cora, his real executive coach, who'd guided him to the place he was now. It was a good place, he realized.

As he was finishing his walk, just as he was about to turn back onto his block, an orange van drove by. He'd seen that van before.

"Hey," he shouted, running into the street to get the driver's attention. The van sailed on.

When he got back to his house, he grabbed his car keys from the kitchen table.

Not five minutes later, he was heading up that winding driveway to the big house where he'd first met the compost kid. He saw all the same things as before. The mansion on the manicured grounds. The carefully tended row of fruit trees. The large, derelict shed off to the side with a jumble of compost bins in front. The sign wasn't up anymore, though. It was leaning against the shed. And he could see by the untamed bushes beyond that the labyrinth behind it had seen better days. He got out of his car and was looking around when someone came out of the house.

"Can I help you?" a man who looked older than Todd said.

"Sorry to bother you," Todd said. "I was just looking for Compost Boy. I saw his orange van earlier this morning."

"Compost Boy?" The man gave him a funny look.

"Are you the husband of the venture capitalist, the one with the son who dropped out of engineering at Stanford to compost?"

"Oh yeah, that kid. He made a composting app and sold it for twenty-five million dollars. Can you believe it?"

"He did?" Todd was stunned.

"No, I'm just kidding," the guy said.

"Oh?" Todd said.

"What really happened is he bought a motorcycle and drove off to Costa Rica. He hasn't been heard from in months!"

"Oh!" Todd said. That hit differently. "Is he okay?"

"No, actually, that didn't happen either."

"What?" Todd said. What was this guy playing at?

"The truth is, I'm just the real estate agent. A Chinese billionaire who's never set foot in the place bought the house. Now it's being sold again. I don't know anything about Compost Boy. Sounds like a fun kid, though."

Todd just stared. His brain was scrambled with all the lives

Compost Boy had lived inside it over the past few minutes.

"Oh," he said. "Well, do you mind if I walk the labyrinth?"

"You mean the maze?"

"Actually, it's a labyrinth," Todd said.

"Huh?" The guy looked at him.

"A maze is full of side paths that don't take you to the end. A labyrinth is just one path. If you follow it, you'll get to the center eventually."

The guy tilted his head. "Not sure I care about any of that at all, but you do you!" Turning around, he went back toward the house.

This time, when Todd walked the labyrinth, he went slower than he had the year before. He wasn't trying to rush it. He wasn't trying to peer around corners to prevent getting lost, as he had before. He understood it for what it was: It wasn't out to trick him, and he'd get to the center eventually. When he got there, he saw the bench he remembered and the fountain with the birdbath. There was a kid's easel propped up that hadn't been there before. From the back of it, Todd could tell it had seen better days. He sat down on the bench.

"Are you the guy who was lost?"

The voice came from behind him. It was the real estate agent. He'd followed him in, and he'd almost given Todd a heart attack in the process.

"You scared me half to death!"

"Are you the one who was lost?"

Todd was getting tired of this weird guy making no sense. "I don't know what you're talking about. I'm not lost. I live right there," he gestured in the direction of his street. "I'm home, man."

The real estate agent pointed to the back of the easel. "Don't shoot the messenger." He raised his hands and backed out behind the curve of the first hedge.

Todd got up to turn the easel around. That's when he saw the message scrawled across the front in permanent marker.

Are you the one who was lost?

There was a lone arrow.

CHAPTER 42

"Hello, unemployed person!" Ray said as soon as Todd logged into the Zoom call.

"Hello!" Todd said.

"Hold on a second," Ray said, pulling Raybot onto the screen. "There's something we always do at the end of every coaching assignment."

"It's my favorite part," Raybot said, looking oddly congenial.

In unison, the robot and the man screamed, "WE WERE WORTH IT?"

As soon as they stopped laughing, Raybot gave Todd a funny look. Then he looked back at Ray. "I thought you said he'd look sad?"

Ray made an awkward noise. "Not sad, glad. GLAD. I said *GLAD*." He turned to Todd. "Raybot's getting on in years." He held up three fingers. "Some of his faculties aren't what they used to be." Now he pointed to his ears.

"I am a little sad," Todd said. "But not in a bad way. I had an amazing decade at LUNAQ, and, in some ways, it would have been great to continue. But it's going to be great to do something else. And I'm not leaving entirely. I'll still be on the board for a while."

Raybot looked at him and then turned to Ray. "I don't believe a word," he mumbled.

"Enough!" Ray said. And then, more forcefully, "Do you want me to turn you off?"

"You wouldn't dare," Raybot said.

"I would!" Ray said.

As their bickering escalated, Todd's phone rang. It was Cora.

"Did you guys already get started?" she said.

"In a way," Todd said, looking at his computer screen as Ray threw a glass of kombucha on his protégé.

Now there was wailing. "You hit me!" The robot was moaning. "And I'm all wet!"

"How deep in are you already?" Cora said.

"Oh, we're in deep," Todd said.

"Well, tell them to stop debriefing until they let me out of the waiting room. I'm your real coach! And I'm just sitting here."

"I'll try," Todd said.

Dripping, Raybot reappeared on Todd's screen. "Do you see what he's done to me?"

Ray swatted at the robot.

"Uh, that was Cora," Todd said. "She said she's just sitting in the waiting room?"

"Where?" Ray said, looking around his office.

"The waiting room, you dolt!" Raybot said. "It's inside the computer!" Now Ray was really confused. Raybot turned to Todd. "This man and his privilege! The best executive coach in the world, and he doesn't even know what a Zoom waiting room is! You know why? Because I take care of everything! I serve it all up on a silver platter. And yet I get absolutely no—"

"Can you guys do this later?" Todd cut in. "Cora's waiting."

"Sure," Ray said. He looked at Raybot expectantly.

"I'm not lifting a finger," Raybot said. "Not until you apologize."

"Apologize for what? You running your mouth?! I say one thing about Todd's precarious mental state, and you're all *blah blah blah*. You need to apologize to me—"

"Later?" Todd said again.

Begrudgingly, Raybot clicked a button. "But I'm not doing this for you," he said to Ray. "I'm doing this for Cora." And then, his voice breaking, "But even so, a thank you would be nice."

The robot's tears hit Ray right where it hurt, and the coach immediately softened. "Come on now, Raybot, is it really as bad as all that?"

"Yes! Do you ever stop to think about how much I've done to make you into the man you are?"

Ray looked up at the ceiling, his own emotions starting to get the better of him now. "You're right," he said. "I don't want to have to deal with Zoom waiting rooms." He took a breath. "And I am privileged to have you in my life. Thank you, Raybot. For everything."

Raybot turned toward Ray, tears now freely flowing. "You really do need me." Ray draped his arms awkwardly over the monitor of the computer-on-wheels.

"What have I walked into?" Cora, whose face had just popped up, said.

"Don't ask me," Todd said. "They started the call by screaming at me. It all seemed to go downhill from there."

"Oh, right. The scream. So, we were?" she said. "Worth it?"

Todd looked from Cora and her beverages to Ray and his crying, dripping robot. He thought about all the good ways he had transformed in the past year and how his life had changed positively along with it. None of it would have happened without them.

Todd nodded his head. "Absolutely."

APPENDIX

KEY TAKEAWAYS

Here are some of the most salient teachings from *Why Can't They Be Like Me?*

On Success
If you want to climb the ladder of success, you better make sure you're climbing the right ladder for you!

On Bouncing Back
When something hard happens, take time to first feel the emotions. Then, and only then, move forward.

On Ideas
Bad ideas can lead to great ideas. So, keep having more of them!

On Transparency

There's a difference between transparency and boundaries. There's a reason we wear clothes in supermarkets, and there's a reason we don't meet our kid's teacher and immediately tell them about all our marital problems. Learn the difference.

On Goal Setting

Goal setting is essential. That said, be careful of becoming so focused on a specific goal that you can't see anything else, including the big picture.

On Operating at the Speed of Trust

As Stephen M.R. Covey explained, the more you trust someone, the faster you can work together to make things happen.*

On Having a Growth Mindset

Carol Dweck's research shows the difference between a fixed mindset, the idea that we have innate traits and can't change or grow, and a growth one, where we can always develop and better ourselves. Believe in growth!†

On Decisions

There's just as much risk in making a decision as there is in not making one.

---

* Stephen M. R. Covey, *The Speed of Trust: The One Thing That Changes Everything* (Free Press, 2008).

† Carol S. Dweck, *Mindset: The New Psychology of Success* (Ballantine Books, 2007).

On Decision-Makers

If you want to influence the decision-maker, treat them like a customer.*

On Apologies

Say sorry. Take accountability. Then, use optimism to transition to the future. (And don't do it again!)

On Regrets

Without the choices you've made, you wouldn't be you. The key to banishing regret is to make peace with your past and live fully in your present.

On Winning Too Much

What's the best thing that can happen to a leader who's always winning? A crisis. There's nothing like a good, raging dumpster fire to turn a good leader into a great one.

On Yes Men (and Women)

The more successful a leader becomes, the more Yes Men magically sprout up around them. Yes Men are other people—senior leaders, employees, friends—who never challenge the leader. That's why the higher a leader rises, the less real dissent they hear. If you're a leader, beware!

---

* This concept comes from Peter Drucker's *The Practice of Management.* Peter F. Drucker, *The Practice of Management* (Harper Business, 2006).

On Change

People *can* change. It takes internal motivation, and a lot of work, but people do it all the time.

On *Becoming Coachable*

Coaching is a great option to help make a change in your life. As outlined in *Becoming Coachable,* there are four key stages to change with the support of a coach: being open to change, being open to feedback, being open to action, and being open to accountability.

On Feedback

Say thank you ;)

On Predictability

The only predictable thing about life is that it's unpredictable.

On Life

Life is good. Breathe!

ABOUT THIS BOOK

Marshall Goldsmith, known as the world's best executive coach, serves as the inspiration for all the good parts of executive coach Ray de Luca.

(And absolutely none of the bad parts!)

The structure of this parable and the journey of Todd Turner's transformation through executive coaching is based on the framework of *Becoming Coachable: Unleashing the Power of Executive Coaching to Transform Your Leadership and Life*, by Marshall Goldsmith, Scott Osman, and Jacquelyn Lane.

Scott Osman and Jacquelyn Lane are the founders of 100 Coaches, the premier executive coaching firm supporting value-creating leaders.

ABOUT THE AUTHORS

Claire Díaz-Ortiz, a partner at 100 Coaches, is a celebrated author and leadership expert who was an early employee at Twitter. *Wired* called her "The Woman Who Got the Pope on Twitter," and *Fast Company* named her one of the 100 Most Creative People in Business. Claire is the author of ten books that have been translated into eleven languages, including *One Minute Mentoring* (coauthored with Ken Blanchard). Claire was named to the Thinkers50 Radar list of emerging management thinkers, and holds an MBA and other degrees from Stanford and Oxford.

Marshall Goldsmith is the founder of the Marshall Goldsmith Group and 100 Coaches. The inaugural winner of the Lifetime Achievement Award for Leadership by the Institute of Coaching at Harvard Medical School and a Thinkers50 Hall of Fame inductee, he is also a professor of management at the Dartmouth Tuck School of Business and a board member for the Peter Drucker Foundation. He received his PhD from the UCLA Anderson School of Management. In his coaching practice, he has advised more than 200 major CEOs and their management teams. Marshall is the author or editor of more than thirty-five books, including *What Got You Here Won't Get You There* and *The Earned Life: Lose Regret, Choose Fulfillment*, written with Mark Reiter.

ABOUT 100 COACHES

---

100 Coaches Agency is the industry leader in bespoke executive coaching services.

In partnership with Marshall Goldsmith, the most renowned executive coach, we've built the world's premier network of executive coaches serving Fortune 500 companies and market-leading organizations. With our carefully curated network of senior-level executive coaches and our proprietary Matchcraft™ process, we deliver precision-matched executive coaching that drives results.

To learn more, visit us online at 100coaches.com.